# How To Write For Television

# How To Write For Television
## by Michelle E. Coe

A HERBERT MICHELMAN BOOK

*Crown Publishers, Inc.*
*New York*

Inquiries should be addressed to
Crown Publishers, Inc.
One Park Avenue
New York, New York 10016

Printed in the United States of America

Published simultaneously in Canada by
General Publishing Company Limited


**Library of Congress Cataloging in Publication Data**

Coe, Michelle E.
How to write for television.

"A Herbert Michelman book."
Includes index.
1. Television authorship.   I. Title.
PN1992.7.C58     1980     808' .025     80-12739
ISBN: 0-517-538504


10 9 8 7 6 5 4 3 2 1

First Edition

*To*
*Margaret Farrar*
*without whose confidence,*
*encouragement*
*and total support*
*this book would not*
*have been written*

# Contents

# How To
# Write For
# Television

# · 1 ·  Introduction

When Ohio University invited me to join the faculty as a part-time instructor in writing for radio and television, I wrote a series of lectures based on my experiences—good and bad—in agencies and stations, and this book is a written version of those lectures.

I want to teach you as much as can be taught about writing, so my book is a primer written in the full knowledge that there is no easy way and that the best instruction comes from doing the job.

Everyone who aspires to any kind of writing knows that he or she is never alone. Always there is the notebook, the constant companion in which you file your thoughts, plots, picturesque speech and interesting situations. The daily journal or diary may not be in vogue, but it is still the best way to record events, thoughts, ideas and your own development. Learn to observe people carefully, how they talk, act and their personal characteristics. Be aware of the drives and motivations of other people. Read, read, read and watch television commercials, documentaries, news and a sprinkling of drama for television. Stay away from theories about advertising and broadcasting while making certain that, through trade magazines and as many contacts in the business as you can accumulate, you are aware of trends. Never assume that your listener knows what you mean when you write obliquely. Just tell your listener and viewer what you want to say. That's singular. You are talking to one person even though the ratings say you talk to thousands.

The most successful writers in radio and televison are those who are able to depart from the present or familiar way of saying and doing things. Writing is a combination of craftsmanship and creativity, but most of all it is writing about what you know best. You've heard that before, but it cannot be emphasized too much.

A few years ago, the creative director's pet in an agency was given an assignment to do a commercial for a perfume. It wasn't even a French perfume, but she wrote about how every whiff would make one think of a walk along the Seine. This woman took the subway from the Bronx to Manhattan every day and spent two weeks on Fire Island in the summertime, but she was writing about walking along the Seine. I've walked along the Seine amid the wine bottles and the fresh urine and that smell is not something I want

1

to dab on my pulse points. Nothing could dissuade the creative director that it wasn't the greatest commercial ever written and he's still wondering why the agency lost the account.

If you are writing about a product, KNOW the product.

1.  What does your product do?
2.  Is your product better than the competition? Why?
3.  Has something been added or deleted that makes it better?
4.  How is the product made?
5.  What other similar products are on the market?
6.  Are these products made differently? How?
7.  What are the real differences in your product?
8.  Why should anyone buy your product rather than another?
9.  Who's watching when your commercial is aired?
10. To whom do you want to sell the product?
11. Where can the product be purchased?
12. Will the viewer buy the product more than once?
13. Does the product appeal to the senses?
14. Does the product boost the ego?
15. Does the viewer need the product? Why?

You write commercials to convince people. Once you have the facts, make an outline of the points you wish to make. Then THINK. Make your own private survey. Talk to people who are objective and have some knowledge of the *category* of your product. Find out what is important to them in the kind of product about which you are writing. This will help you to emphasize the more important features and play down others.

If you are writing an editorial, it is vital that you know both sides of the issue so you can present a full story even though you will be presenting a point of view.

If you are writing news, the first rule is accuracy, and if you intend to present a commentary or analysis, your research is doubly important.

If you are a total blank, don't just quit and do nothing. Read something light and distracting; take a nap or go for a walk and come back to it. Put down anything that comes into your head, sketch or better still, tape-record a personal pitch to a close friend. Play it back. Do you believe what you said? If you do, you are on the right track.

Don't rely on a lucky pair of pants or think you have to be in a certain place under certain circumstances and in a certain mood. All you get out of that is a shiny seat, a blank piece of paper and a self-defeating waste of time.

Experience the joy of your own creativity. You can.

# ▪ 2 ▪   Punctuation—Seen and Unseen

A book about writing for television must include the challenges to the performer. It is the actor or actress who will present the concept, mood and message of the writer.

It is not unusual to walk through an advertising agency, station or network and see people typing and seemingly talking to themselves. These are the pros who know that television must be written for the ear as well as the eye. All of radio is written for the ear, but the beginner may be deceived into thinking that television is for the eye only. It is the spoken word and the way it is spoken that makes the reputation of the writer and the believability of the message. Certainly, the skilled television writer makes it easier for the performer. Strange as it may seem, I think every writer for television should take a course in television performance. Only then will he know how to write his copy for the best possible presentation. My personal recommendation for such a course or courses is to be found at the famous Weist-Barron schools. The Weist-Barron schools (there are seven branches from New York to California) are taught by active professionals for professionals, and whether or not the writer intends to become a writer-performer, writer-producer, writer-director or just a writer, he should know how to write copy that seems conversational but is really pseudo-conversational. It becomes conversational only through the professional presentation of the trained and experienced actor or actress. In the early days of television, it was said that a television writer could not write for print. If you look at pretelevision print ads and then at print ads of today, you will see that the print writer writes like a television writer. The writer writes.

It's been said that writing is the technology of the work of the mind. In print, the writer seeks to communicate his images, ideas, beliefs, observations, perspectives, desires and perhaps experiences by his choice of words and combinations of words about a given situation, place, person or product. The print writer may seek to entertain, inform or persuade. If the print writer is trying to do the last, he must persuade the buyer by the use of descriptive adjectives related to the needs, hopes, dreams and wishes of the reader.

The radio writer must be well aware that speech is performance and he must write those words that enable the listener to use his own imagination about places and persons. The beauty of radio is that it can conceal the fact that the romantic voice belongs to a man who is five feet tall and four feet wide. The radio writer will not merely mention that you can become a "blond" if you use a certain product but will furnish his on-the-air salesperson with words such as "silken hair flowing like the drippings of golden honey." If you think that's corny, watch some television commercials about hair products and cosmetics. What they don't say, they imply with the video. A well-trained radio salesperson will gleefully seize upon descriptive adjectives and add his own throaty inflections so that the listener can see herself tripping around barefoot with shoulder-length hair the color of golden honey. In the early days of radio, homemakers could dream such dreams and extend them into a private world where she was discovered by a movie producer and made famous and rich. Such reveries were often interrupted by the ringing of the doorbell and the sight of a balding delivery man. No matter. The image remained and on her next trip to the village, the listener would pick up a bottle of the advertised hair dye and believe herself beautiful even if her hair came out looking like a bale of hay.

Radio is the last medium for the use of a beautiful voice. Even that is being discouraged. Since many listeners have voices that are flat, nasal, accented, thin and high or husky and low, performers with just such voices are "cast" to perform commercials. Advertisers believe this helps establish rapport between the viewer and the spokesperson and lends credence to the claims of the product. Gone are the golden-throated announcers and actresses in favor of the performer who can make the listener feel that a friend or close acquaintance is sharing the information with him. Our brains have been dissolved by the use of vulgar or incorrect language and "natural voices." The writer may not have much if anything to say about the casting of the commercial, but he can indicate to his creative director the kind of person and voice that he believes is best related to the product. The first concern of the writer is to sell the product. This must be done in the most subtle manner. After all, your commercial is interrupting a discussion of important governmental affairs or perhaps a program of music just when the listener is beginning to change his mind or tap his toes. Be polite and direct without being aggressive. It's a great temptation for a writer to write an award-winning commercial that's so clever the listener forgets the name and purpose of the product or service. An award will look great on your résumé as you trudge around looking for a job after you've been bounced out of your former position for forgetting that you are selling—not entertaining. Define your objective first.

Are you attracting attention; giving information; proving a point or providing a variation of an old idea as a reminder? Know what you are trying to do. Know to whom you are projecting the commercial and where that person is likely to be.

In television the scene is set. No more fanciful picturing for the viewer. There it is . . . and there goes the use of that wonderful faculty of imagination. The characters on the screen are young, beautiful and intelligent. Middle-aged and old are presented as caricatures. We hope this will change.

Be ethical enough to tell the truth about your product and realize that no product and no commercial is pleasing to everyone.

As it is, viewers infer a lot that isn't shown or said. Notice the difference in these selling messages for print, radio and television.

For print:

Every woman needs GYNOGEN whether she is young, middle-aged or older. GYNOGEN is a gentle internal cleanser that was formulated by a well-known gynecologist. GYNOGEN maintains the correct acid-alkaline balance that is so important and keeps you free from bacteria and fungus infections that can cause itching and irritation. GYNOGEN is odorless and protective and keeps you clean, refreshed and safe. GYNOGEN is the internal cleanser for your health, your security and your protection.

For radio:

Health care is important for everyone, but women have particular needs. Every woman . . . young . . . middle-aged and older . . . needs GYNOGEN. Internal cleansing is important for the acid-alkaline balance that stops itching and irritation. GYNOGEN is the medically approved formula that fights bacteria and fungus infections. Get GYNOGEN. Formulated by a well-known gynecologist . . . GYNOGEN is odorless and protective. Get GYNOGEN today . . . for your health's sake.

That's the way you write it if the commercial is performed "live" by an announcer or the MC of a classical musical show. Live performance is still used in some markets and on some stations. More often, the commercial is recorded and the "live" person will say: "We'll be back with more news after this important message," or "We'll resume our concert after we bring you this word . . . [or this information]." If the message is recorded, you can hit them in the eardrums immediately after they have been alerted that a commercial is coming . . . like this:

> GYNOGEN is important for every woman who cares about her health and protection. GYNOGEN is the safe, gentle internal cleanser that women of every age need. To maintain the correct acid-alkaline balance, use GYNOGEN. Formulated by a well-known gynecologist, GYNOGEN relieves itching and irritation often caused by bacteria and fungus infections. Get GYNOGEN today and take care of yourself.

No nonsense about the last one. The product is mentioned five times; its usage is well defined; a promise has been made and the listener did not have to wait for a buildup. She was waiting for a commercial, she expected to be sold something and she hears it even if she's impatient to hear the rest of the news or the next selection of music.

In television you will first write the commercial before consultation with the art director with whom you will work in getting the commercial on storyboard. Since we are talking about writing now, we will come to storyboard later. Initially, your commercial will look like this:

### ALLEN-WILEY,   Advertising

---

Client:   Bailey-Edward Laboratories
Date:
Product:   GYNOGEN
Writer:   Your name

| VIDEO | AUDIO |
|---|---|
| MCU* YOUNG WOMAN IN MID-THIRTIES. | Young, middle-aged or older, every woman needs GYNOGEN. For gentle, internal cleansing that maintains the correct acid-alkaline balance . . . use GYNOGEN. Formulated by a well-known gynecologist, GYNOGEN keeps you free of bacteria and fungus infections that can cause itching and irritation. |

*MCU: Medium close-up (see Terminology).

| | |
|---|---|
| CUT TO ECU* OF GYNOGEN BOX. | Odorless, protective—GYNOGEN keeps you clean, refreshed and safe. |
| CUT TO MCU† WOMAN HOLDING BOX OF GYNOGEN. | GYNOGEN. For your health, your security and your protection. |

In the television commercial, the copy has more flow and can be spoken with sincerity and naturalness. Most of all, there is definite, pointed information presented with a minimum of words. Yet all of the message is there with the added persuasion of the action verb *use*. Action verbs are the essence of television commercials. The viewer is urged to DO something. Use. Ask for. Buy. Take. Eat.

It is hoped that the television commercial writer will recognize his work for what it really is . . . consumer service. Commercials are not made just to make money for the manufacturer and the network or station. Commercials are made to give information, consumer service or to bring attention to a worthwhile cause or organization that needs help.

The television writer of commercials should strive to see that his advertising message has flow, enthusiasm, sincerity, naturalness of expression and definite pointed information. Avoid rambling. Even though the creative director, the account executive or the client insists upon the mention of all of the virtues of the product, it is best to have one strong selling point. Perhaps a cleaning product does wash, disinfect, deodorize and resist dirt, but the video cannot depict all of them. Mention what is required, but emphasize that feature of the product that excels a similar competitive product.

Writers for television must be conscious of what a voice can do with minimal difficulty. It is the responsibility of the actor or actress to speak well, but the television writer can work for the performer by remembering the pitfalls of alliteration. Few performers are born with perfect articulation. The performer knows and the writer must be aware that microphones magnify such consonants as *t, b, p* and *s*. The performer has to learn how to speak without popping, blowing and hissing into the microphone. The writer can make it easier for the performer to voice the words of the creator if he is aware of the use and combinations of words that ensure a natural, conversational delivery.

Would you write any of the following lines for a performer?

*ECU: Extreme close-up (see Terminology).
†MCU: Medium close-up (see Terminology).

Choose cool school shoes.
Clean, crisp, crimson currants.
Chicken, steaks and chops.
Severonson's sharp shears snip seventy slim shingles.
Starch shirts stiff.
Stevens statistical stamper sticks stamps.
Blacker's black bric-a-brac.
Frozen fresh Swiss fish.
Tie three tree twigs tightly.
Barton's better butter made better batter for better bread.
Peel pears properly.
Timmy's ten thin tin tongs took turkey from the terrace.
Skirts, shirts, sweaters.
A smart fellow felt smart.
The sheet was split but here I sit.
Pluck figs with the fig plucker.
Sell a school coal scuttle.
Tutor two fluters to toot the flute.

While these examples may seem exaggerated, the writer should experiment by trying to say each sentence three times rapidly and he will become conscious of the importance of his choice of words to be spoken.

The creative writer in any area of television may be frustrated and confused, since it is too often true that he does not have full control. The writer of commercials in an advertising agency may get his direction from the creative director, who received his direction from the account executive who may or may not accurately interpret the goals of the advertiser. The commercial may have many "fingers in the pie," including those of the advertiser's wife, the casting director and the producer.

The writer of the presentation for a new program may have to cope with the vague and fuzzy ideas of the creator if the idea is not his own. Even then, the potential buyer may ask for innumerable changes until the original idea is lost.

The news writer is subject to the assignment editor and to the producer. That which the writer knows will add depth and excitement to his story may be eliminated because of the time allotted for a particular item.

The serial writer works under a group head whose idea of the development of a story line may be different from or even inferior to his conception, and subject to deletions by the producer.

The writer of the narrative may find his sequential order changed by flashbacks.

The writer of the documentary may be asked to make certain

fictional additions that of course destroy the authenticity of the documentary.

Flexibility, willingness to take direction and the ability to work under pressure without developing an ulcer are required of the writer for television.

There doesn't seem to be any way to improve the pronunciation of the writer's words, but perhaps good rapport with the producer can help to eliminate some of the sounds that make writers cringe.

How often do we hear *length* pronounced as *lenth?* *Long Island* becomes *Long Guyland. Height* is pronounced *highth* and *often* is often heard as *off-ten. White* comes off *wite.* We can't put the correct pronounciation in parenthesis in the copy, but how we wish we might!

The writer needs to be constantly aware of the talents and limitations of the performer. If the writer has the advantage of knowing the actor or actress who will speak his words and interpret his intentions and mood, he can write "to" or capture the uniqueness of the performer. The writer should have a definite character concept, which is made known in his choice of words and continuity of thought. The casting director and/or producer will determine which of many persons will actually play the part or perform the commercial. The results are sometimes amazing, but the skills of the writer can contribute to the suitability of the spokesperson and the material.

# ▪ 3 ▪    On or Off the Mark?

Recent surveys prove that some people never read books, a few read occasionally and very few read regularly. But a large majority watches television regularly. From television, they learn how to speak and it is the responsibility of the television writer to know what is correct and what is not. The trained performer can speak correct English until it sounds perfectly natural, yet some advertisers and producers will resist this with the often-heard phrase, "But people don't talk like that." Not all television viewers are illiterate or careless, and in subtle ways, the television writer and indeed the industry can eliminate criticism and upgrade the communication of viewers by following a few simple basic rules.

Isn't it just as easy to write different "from" as it is to write the incorrect different "than"? Yet, how many times do you hear the most highly paid commentators say "different *than*"? Please. Do one little thing. Write "Different FROM."

Here are some other reminders:

A picture is hung. A person is hanged.

*At* concerns a definite time. *About* is indefinite. You would never write "at about five o'clock." You would write "at five o'clock" or "about five o'clock."

"Over" is used with people. "More than" is used with numbers. For example:

> Over two hundred people attended.
> More than three million dollars was pledged during the telethon.

You climb a mountain. You don't climb up a mountain. If you are climbing, you are going up.

The word *farther* refers to physical space. For example:

> I am going farther.

The word *further* has to do with time, degree or quantity. For example:

> Further information will be available tomorrow.

*Farther* and *further* are frequently used interchangeably, but the distinction is important to the careful writer.

The word *only* is constantly misused and yet the correct usage adds color and emphasis. *Only* is put before the word it modifies. Most often one hears, "I only had bus fare." Are you really the only person who had bus fare? Are you saying that you had enough money for bus fare and nothing more? Then the correct, "I had only bus fare" emphasizes your plight and states the true meaning of what you wanted to say.

Many television writers use *imply* and *infer* interchangeably. *Imply* is the word to use when something is indicated. *Imply* is a hint, suggestion or intimation. *Infer* is used when a person concludes or decides something that is known or assumed. For example: "I infer that he is pleased with the result." You don't know that he is really pleased, but actions or facial expressions give that impression and so you *infer* that he is pleased. A political speaker may hint that he believes in a larger defense budget without actually saying so. In that case, he implied as much. Yet one well-known writer-commentator continues to express his personal *inferences* as the statements of the person he has interviewed. Constantly, this writer-speaker presumes to present the position of the world-famous leaders about whom he speaks as, "He inferred that there would be large budget cuts" when "he" hadn't done anything of the sort. "He" implied that. The writer-commentator who interviewed him *inferred* it.

Sports announcers are often heard saying, "Mr. Jones has just presented the winner *with* a check." You don't need *with*.

Use fewer words. Save your energy. Write quite simply, "Mr. Jones has presented the winner a check."

*As* and *so* are often misunderstood. Some people use *so* with the thought that they appear to be educated. They do not seem to know that *as* is used in affirmative comparisons and so is used in negative comparisons.

For example:

> Jennifer is as pretty as Elizabeth.
> Jennifer is not so pretty as Elizabeth.

All it really takes is a little thought. One beloved television writer-commentator reveals the gaps in his education by constantly saying "he don't," "she don't." If he thought about it, would he say, "he do not" or "she do not"? Surely, he would say "doesn't."

Please write "this kind" or "these kinds." Not "this kinds" or "these kind."

Have you heard anyone say, "He had came into the room"? *Came* is never used with have, has or had.

Hollywood made its contribution to our speech corruption with the contracted "Whodunit" to describe a mystery film. It's too late now to call mystery films "Who did it," but the most macho detectives in television series do not walk to the scene of a crime and say, "Who done it?" They may chew gum, chomp a cigar or talk with their mouths full of lollipops or pastrami sandwiches, but they follow the script and say, "Who did it?"

Haven't you heard, "I have swam in the lake"? "I haven't wrote him yet" and worst of all, "We have drank the wine." The correct use of the word *drunk* in the last sentence doesn't make a potential alcoholic.

A television writer informs, entertains, and yes—he teaches. The viewer imitates the performer. The performer presents and interprets the creativity and knowledge of the writer.

Then there's that trouble with *was* and *were*.

After a singular subject preceded by IF, use the word *was* when expressing a fact.

For example:

> If he was there, why didn't he come to the phone? (He was there.)
> If she was ill, why didn't she say so? (She was ill.)

If you are showing a condition contrary to fact, however, use *were* after IF.
For example:

> If I were you, I should go. (I am not you.)
> If Jack were here, he would help us. (Jack is NOT here.)

With plural subjects always use *were.*
For example:

> If *they* were annoyed, why didn't they leave?

Avoid confusion with *each other* and *one another. Each other* refers to two persons or things.
For example:

> The boy and dog love each other.

*One another* refers to more than two persons or things.
For example:

> The salesmen competed with one another.

If you are using the word *blame,* follow it by the name of the person or thing. Do not write "Blame it on . . ." Write, "Blame Irving." "Blame greed."

When describing a thing, do not write, "It was that kind of a hat." Rather write, "It was that kind of hat." Always the fewer words the better.

We've all had the experience of asking, "How are you?" and being told a grocery list of symptoms. If you are writing dialogue and one of your characters asks, "Are you ill?" Let your written answer be "rather" or "somewhat" not "kind of " or "sort of."

Much of your proper usage of grammar will be important in the writing of news, narration, documentaries and episodic and serial presentations.

Never have one of your characters say, "I laid down." Use *lie, lay, lain* or *lying* when you are writing about assuming position. When you are writing about placing something, use *lay, laid* or *laying.* For example: I lay this contract before you for your immediate signature." Or, "I laid the letter on the table in the hall."

In writing of the future use *shall* with I and we. Use *will* with other persons—he, she, you, they.

In writing to express promise, threat, determination or consent, use *will* with I and we, but use *shall* with all other subjects.

Remember that *can* denotes power or ability and *may* denotes permission or possibility. It is just as easy to write into a television commercial for a child who wants more breakfast cereal: "May I have some more, please?" as it is to be incorrect and folksy with, "Can I have some more, Mom?" Children's Action for Television will notice and they are a powerful influence on the agencies, networks and the Federal Communications Commission.

If you are writing a teen-age sequence, please have your female character say, "He and I went to the movies," not "Him and me."

*Between* refers to a discourse or situation between two persons and *among* is used for more than two persons.

After the comparatives *else, other, otherwise, rather* or *hardly,* use the word *than.* Never use *but* or *when.* For example: "Hardly had the snow ended than the rain and sleet came."

Make clear distinctions for the commercial spokesperson or the actor or actress in a drama. *Affect* means to influence, to pretend or to act upon. "I was affected by the unexpected altitude of Mexico City." "She affected a southern accent." *Effect* as a noun means a result. "She suffered from the effects of sun exposure." *Effect* as a verb means to bring about, accomplish or produce. "The doctor effected a cure." "The manager effected a change in the personnel department." *Healthy* means having good health. *Healthful* means health-giving. For example: "The doctor prescribed a healthful diet." *Exceptional* means rare or unusual while *exceptionable* indicates that which is liable to exception. *Loath* means unwilling (I was loath to go). Add an *e* to make it *loathe* and it means to hate or abhor. (I loathe mice.) *Happen* means to occur or take place, but *transpire* means to become known. In today's television world, you are unlikely to use the word *transpire* unless you become a writer for a political figure who issues political statements. If you are writing a demonstration food commercial, or a script for a gourmet cook, simply write that you, "cut an apple in two" or "in halves." Don't write, "And now you cut the apple in half."

I know what you are going to think and what you will encounter, but wouldn't it be nice if we could hear a soap opera performer say quite naturally, "It's I?" I doubt that we shall. It's probably going to remain, "It's me," but in other instances when you use a subject form on one side of the verb *to be,* you must use a subject form on the other side. You can write "I'm she," unless your character is a barefoot abandoned child and then I suppose the producer will insist upon "I'm her." Use the subject form with the verb *be* (am, is, are, was, were) only when it is used as the MAIN verb. However, a form of *be* may be a "helping" verb. "It is hurting me" (not I) because "hurting" is the main verb.

News writers are expected to be educated people who speak to educated people. A news writer knows that a criminal suspect is arraigned. He is not *arranged*. *Who* is the object form (who was elected?) and *whom* is the subject of a verb or preposition. (Whom did you ask for?) *Real* means genuine. *Really* means actually and *very* means exceedingly. There is a distinction, so please make it. When you are writing in the comparative, you are writing about two things. "He is the taller of the twins." In the superlative you are writing of more than two, "Washington was the wisest of our presidents."

As a television writer, you will be constantly conscious of action verbs. Television is the instant communicator and the instant is now. Remember that verbs of the five senses are followed by adjectives unless they mean action.

For example:

I feel very bad about it.
She sang badly.
Your cough sounds bad.
I hurt my arm badly.
She looks slow. (She is slow.)
The roses smell sweet. (They are sweet.)
The man stood [that is, no action] quiet.

Many writers don't think about the very basics of writing, but it's just as important to remember them in television as it is in print. An adjective is descriptive of a noun. An adverb may modify a verb, an adjective or another adverb and it tells how, when or where. (He went quickly.) A pronoun must agree with its antecedent in person, number and gender. (Everyone has his own troubles.) (The committee brought in its report.)

Finally, know what you mean and mean what you say. Many words sound almost the same, such as *elicit*, which means to draw out, and *illicit*, which refers to that which is improper or unlawful. Other words don't sound the same but are often used interchangeably. One example of this is the use of *fewer* and *less*. *Fewer* refers to things that can be counted and *less* refers to bulk. (I called no fewer than ten times.) (I should prefer less praise and fewer duties.)

By all means learn to spell. It is amazing how many slides on television contain misspelled words. Poor spelling in a commercial or any script can be disastrous. If you spell *accidentally* as *accidently*, the careless or minimally trained commentator will pronounce it as he sees it. The writer is the word master. No matter what happens to the copy after it leaves the writer, at least there is the pride of craftsmanship.

Punctuation may be less important in television writing than in print. It is the performer under the direction of the client, director and producer who will provide the unwritten punctuation. But the writer should provide the minimal basics. A period marks the end of a declarative or imperative sentence. A comma is used to separate the units of a series. A semicolon separates expressions that are not closely related enough to be separated by periods. A colon is a sign of introduction. (The slogan was: Pay as you go.)

The safest rule for the successful writer of television is to follow a general outline of idea, attitude, mood and most of all, the ability to write in a sequence of different thoughts. If the television writer follows that formula, he becomes a partner with the performer who will present his words.

# ▪ 4 ▪ Radio and Television Copy Rules

1. Always use a heavy stock paper. Onionskin is not heavy enough. It can be used for the second copy.

2. Double-space all copy for radio and all dialogue in television.

3. Type dialogue (the spoken word) for both radio and television in lower case and caps. *Do not type in all caps.*

4. Type directions like SOUND or MUSIC, ANNOUNCER in all caps. This separates it from the dialogue. Do this even though the direction is in the AUDIO column.

5. Always include at the top of the material your name, the date, the assignment and the length of the copy.

6. Don't hand in copy with obvious errors. This shows you failed to proofread your material.

7. Television copy should utilize the split page. The audio generally goes on the right-hand side of the page, the video on the left.

8. For radio, you utilize the whole page, separating audio from the directions by using all caps for the directions; i.e., ANNOUNCER, (LOUDLY), DOOR CLOSING, etc.

9. Never hyphenate any word on direction on a commercial or script.

# ▪ 5 ▪    The Video Page

On the following page you will see a sample video page. Some agencies will have a heading that uses the company name, while other headings read "Television Copy" or "Draft Copy." None will have the word *Video* on the left half of the page and the word *Audio* on the right half. You're supposed to know that. Too many don't indicate what is put on what line and the sheet merely looks like this:

Jane Jones
June 16, 1977
EARLY BIRD BREAKFAST BARS
Tilson Foods
20 seconds

| VIDEO | AUDIO |
|---|---|
| ECU* GIRL IN LIVING ROOM. | I live alone and keep my schedule as free as I can. |
| CUT TO MCU GIRL BEFORE KITCHEN CUPBOARD. | I want to be able to accept or offer a last-minute invitation to dinner. |
| CUT TO CU GIRL HOLDING BOX OF CRANE MACARONI AND CHEESE. | That's why I always have CRANE Macaroni and Cheese in my cupboard. Friends stop by and I'm always ready with CRANE Macaroni and Cheese. |
| CUT TO SEQUENCE OF CU'S OF CASSEROLES. | I can serve it plain; mix it with tuna, crabmeat or salmon . . . maybe some peas and carrots. |
| CUT TO CU OF GIRL WITH BOX OF CRANE MIX. | Your friend for friends is macaroni and cheese . . . |
| CUT TO SMILING GIRL. SUPER CRANE LOGO | by CRANE, of course. |

# ▪ 6 ▪   Terminology

Since the television and the radio writer must know the signals from the control room, floor manager, and what the camera can and cannot do, the following list of the more frequently used terms is included.

*See Terminology for camera directions.

| | |
|---|---|
| AD LIB | To speak without a script or to say lines not written in the script. |
| ANNC | When the announcer speaks. |
| ANNCR | The announcer. |
| BILLBOARD | Sponsor's logo or identification or list of attractions on show. |
| BLACK OUT | Go out of a scene and into total black. |
| BRIDGE | Music played to carry a change of scene, mood or situation. |
| COLD | To start a program or announcement without any preceding announcement, music or sound. |
| CRAWL | A moving roll of credits. |
| CREDITS | The roll of jobs connected with the show and who does them. Always at the end of a show. |
| CROSS FADE | To blend one sound into another by diminishing the volume of the existing sound while at the same time increasing the volume of the sound to follow. |
| CU | Close-up. Head and shoulders. |
| CUE | A hand signal to a performer that tells him to begin. Words, sounds or music that precede a performer's participation. Words that precede the change of a program from one point to another. |
| CUT TO | A fast but smooth switch from one shot to the next. |
| DISSOLVE TO | Exactly what it says. One shot dissolves into a new one. |
| DOLLY IN | Moving camera in toward the person or object being photographed. |
| DOLLY OUT | Moving camera away from the person or object being photographed. |
| ECU | Extreme close-up. Head or maybe just one feature, i.e., eyes, mouth or nose. |
| EXT | Exterior. Always followed by a description of the exterior and the time of day. |
| FADE IN | To come up on a scene out of black. |
| FADE OUT | To go out on a scene gradually and go to black. |
| ID | Identification of either the network or station call letters. |
| INT | Interior. Includes description and time of day. |
| LAP DISSOLVE | A technique in which the picture on a camera or slide projector is faded from full to black while at the same time a picture from another source is faded from black to full. |
| MCU | Medium close-up. Waist and head shot. |

| | |
|---|---|
| MONTAGE | A series of three or more pictures in fairly rapid succession that is done by superimposing one picture over another by means of dissolves. |
| PAN | Turn the camera on a horizontal line in a sweeping motion. |
| PROMO | A promotional announcement about the station or one of its programs. |
| PSA | Public Service Announcement broadcast at the expense of the station in behalf of a nonprofit charitable organization. |
| SEGUE | A selection of music going into another selection without interruption. |
| 2 SHOT | Two people in the frame. |
| 3 SHOT | Three people in the frame. |
| 4 SHOT | Four people in the frame. |
| SFX | Sound effects. Always followed by a specific, such as "horses hooves." |
| SOF | Sound on film. What is seen is accompanied by sound. |
| STOCK SHOTS | Filmed scenes taken of people, objects, structures or sites or portions of motion pictures that are on file for reuse. |
| SUPER | Putting one visual on top of another. |
| TILT | The camera moves on its axis in a vertical direction whether up or down. |
| TITLES | The name of the show, names of stars, writers, producers, etc. |
| TRACK OR TRUCK | The camera moves from left to right and always along a horizontal line. |
| UNDER | To play the music at a low volume and keep it playing while someone speaks or there is some other sound. |
| UNDER AND OUT | To play the music at a low volume under other sound and then fade it out entirely. |
| VO | Voice over. Someone who is not seen speaks. |
| WIDE SHOT | A shot some distance from the object or person being photographed that encompasses the surroundings. |
| WIPE | A control technique where one picture is replaced by another and the new picture crowds off the first by pushing it off to one side, to the top or bottom. |
| ZOOM | The lens of the camera moves in or out from wide to close-up or vice versa. |

## ▪ 7 ▪          The Code

In addition to knowing how to do it, the writer for radio and television must know what he can and cannot do, and so it seems well to include some of the basic rules of the NAB code. The National Association of Broadcasters has established certain regulations that attempt to ensure better service to the public and certain standards and practices toward that end. Because of this, the writer has to know what he can and cannot say. As you know, there is no cigarette advertising on radio or television; nor is there any advertising of hard liquor. Wine and beer, yes, but you will never see anyone consuming beer or wine on a television commercial. Look closely. You will see bottles and glasses waved in the air, glasses clinked and beverages poured, but no one actually drinks in a commercial except a make-believe sip. Other current no-no's are: Insecticides are never shown being used in the presence of pets or children. No fortune-telling or occultism, and many rules about astrology. No promotion of betting or lotteries by tip sheets. No advertisers with two products can use the copy of one acceptable product to promote the brand name of an unacceptable product. No bait switch advertising is allowed. In other words, an advertiser cannot urge you to buy one kind of sewing machine and then persuade you to buy another kind when you order. Testimonials are supposed to reflect personal experience, although I sincerely doubt that they do. There is not supposed to be any disparagement of the competition, although I see it every day. Institutions of learning must not exaggerate opportunities for those who enroll. Firearms and ammunition sold by mail are not acceptable in broadcasting. The writer may say "acne" and "blemishes" but may not say "pimples" or "blackheads," and there can be no video showing the condition. There can be no claims that an acne product will work where others fail. Dog food commercials cannot say "hash" or "stew" and they cannot misrepresent the quality or amount of meat in the product. Nor can they say it's a complete food if it is a supplemental. Arthritic sufferers will always hear that a product brings TEMPORARY relief of aches and pains. Medication for arthritis cannot say that the product RESTORES function, nor can it be said that thus and so product is a miracle drug.

When it comes to toys, there are so many consumer protection rules in the code that it would require an entire book to list them. However, no toy can be advertised as JUST five dollars, and there

must be realistic sounds and display performance in the demonstration.

In the health field, there are even more stringent rules in the
code. No performer may wear a white coat AND a stethoscope, and
there must be no video of pill taking for purposes of treatment.

There are violations of the code all of the time, but not every
station subscribes to the code and some of those who do ignore
it. The code keeps changing.

A complete copy of the code can be obtained from the National
Association of Broadcasters in New York or Washington, D.C.

# • 8 •   Concepts and Headlines

If you find yourself working in an advertising agency, the creative
director may insist upon having several concepts and headlines
having to do with the product of the client that is to be used in a
commercial.

A *concept* is an overall general idea about a product.

A *headline* may be more like a slogan than that commonly known
as a headline in the publishing world.

Some few examples are:

> Product:  Hailo Pineapple
>
> Concept:  The variety of things made with or enhanced by
> the use of Hailo Pineapple.
>
> Headline: Hailo makes the best of everything.

> Product:  Charlie's Glue
>
> Concept:  The versatility of Charlie's Glue and its efficacy
> when used to repair wooden, china, vinyl, plastic
> or porcelain objects.
>
> Headline: When your world falls apart . . . Charlie's Glue.

> Product:  Sweetnite Cream
>
> Concept:  A tinted moisturizing cream to wear overnight.
>
> Headline: Make Up and Kiss Goodnight.

Write concepts and headlines for five different products.

1.  A perfume.
2.  A laundry detergent.
3.  An automobile.
4.  A domestic wine.
5.  A deodorant.

You may substitute others if you use five unrelated products.

In print, we may assume the copy is accompanied by a photograph. A printed illustration is static. Without the addition of a radio voice to give personality to the product or the motion of television to give it life, the copy must inform and persuade. Here are two examples of products written for print, radio and television.

For print:

> SHEEN TONE—the revolutionary synthetic cream shampoo made available by Primrose House. SHEEN TONE lathers abundantly in hard or soft water and rinses easily and quickly. SHEEN TONE gives your hair highlights and natural sheen. The economy size jar of SHEEN TONE— $5—at your favorite store.

For radio:

> That revolutionary new beauty aid is here . . . SHEEN TONE . . . the new synthetic cream shampoo, developed and just recently made available by Primrose House, famous New York beauty salon. SHEEN TONE is not a soap . . . it contains nothing that clings to your hair to make it dull and lifeless. SHEEN TONE lathers abundantly in any kind of water, affording several times as much lather as the finest soap shampoo. You can dry your hair more quickly after a SHEEN TONE shampoo, and no special rinse or other extras are necessary. For entrancing hair highlights and natural sheen, buy SHEEN TONE in the five-dollar economy size jar.

For television:

| VIDEO | AUDIO |
|---|---|
| FADE IN | |
| MCU GIRL WITH SHOULDER-LENGTH HAIR. | My hair was dull, dry and lifeless. I used all kinds of shampoos, rinses and conditioners. Nothing helped . . . Until I found |
| MCU GIRL HOLDS JAR. | SHEEN TONE. SHEEN TONE is not a soap . . . it's a new synthetic cream shampoo. |
| CUT TO MCU OF GIRL SHAMPOOING. | SHEEN TONE lathers abundantly in any kind of water and leaves no residue that clings to your hair. You don't |

| | |
|---|---|
| | need special rinses or other extras. |
| CUT TO ECU OF GIRL WITH FINISHED HAIRDO. | SHEEN TONE gives my hair radiant highlights and brings out the natural sheen. Try SHEEN TONE and bring out the beauty of your hair. |
| CUT TO MCU GIRL WITH JAR. | SHEEN TONE by Primrose House. |

For print:

(Photograph of legs in FARGO hosiery and another pair of legs in FARGO pantyhose.)

The way to go is FARGO . . . beautiful stockings and pantyhose from Fargo Mills, the leader in beautiful, sheer wrinkle-free stockings and pantyhose. To take you everywhere . . . beautifully. In all the wanted shades . . . $2.50 for stockings. $4.50 for the pantyhose.

For radio:

You can be the leader wherever you go in FARGO stockings and pantyhose. FARGO makes your legs look beautiful. Sheer . . . comfortable . . . wrinkle-free . . . FARGO hose are always recognized on the best dressed women. Near or far . . . go to your favorite store and ask for FARGO . . . the stockings and pantyhose for leading women.

For television:

# ▪ 9 ▪  The Television Commercial

Jane Jones
FARGO MILLS
FARGO STOCKINGS
Preston and Preston Agency
20 seconds

| VIDEO | AUDIO |
|---|---|
| OPEN ON A PAIR OF BEAUTIFUL LEGS WALKING ALONG A SIDEWALK. | MUSIC: INSTRUMENTAL BALLAD |

CAMERA MOVES WITH GIRL
FOR ABOUT FIVE SECONDS.

ANNCR VO

CUT TO LEGS OF YOUNG
MAN WALKING ALONG
SIDEWALK FOLLOWING GIRL.

Everyone always follows the
leader, and a leader is always
recognized.

CUT TO LONG SHOT
SHOWING GIRL; A
PROCESSION OF MEN
FOLLOWING THE BEAUTIFUL
GIRL.

FARGO has always been a leader
in beautiful hose for beautiful
legs. And sometimes even
not-so-beautiful legs look
beautiful when they're wearing
FARGO. Sheer, wrinkle-free
Fargo makes a leader out of
you.

CUT ECU GIRL'S FACE AS
SHE SMILES.

CUT BACK TO PROCESSION
SHOT. GIRL STOPS AT
PLAYGROUND AND A MAN
AND TWO CHILDREN RUN UP
TO HER. OBVIOUSLY,
HUSBAND AND CHILDREN.
REACTION SHOT MEN'S
FACES.

Because FARGO is always
recognized on the world's most
beautiful legs.

SUPER PRODUCT

SUPER LOGO

Compare the three mediums. In print, we've told you the essential facts about the products and given you an eye-catching reason for wanting to buy them.

In radio, we've added a personal touch with adjectives that the spokesperson can endow with emotion as well as a bit of conversational puffery.

In television, we've shown you a person using the product and drawn you into her personal experience. The matching of the spokesperson to the product is important because viewers to whom the product is projected must identify with her, the problem she solved or the enhancement of her personal appearance by the use of the product(s).

Study these examples and prepare to move on to the presentation of the commercial to a client as you come to the chapter on storyboards. Please remember that the copy is the element of the sale with which you as a writer are concerned. This book is not a book on production and only minimal camera directions are given in the hope that you will exercise your powers of visualization; take a course in production, but learn to live with the fact that the art director, the producer and the director may "see" the commercial quite differently from you. Your task is to put down the words that will best sell the product.

Your success comes as you watch commercials, newscasts, serials, documentaries and, with the help of the glossary of terms, determine what the camera is doing. Your own imagination and visualization will be the greatest help to you in developing your own style and uniqueness rather than merely copying what is already on the air. Storyboards will help you. You can make your own. Draw a series of rectangular squares and sketch in the action as you visualize it. Put your dialogue below each square. Storyboard paper can be bought, but it's an unnecessary expense, at least to start.

# ▪10▪        Storyboard

A storyboard is the equivalent of a building contractor's blueprint. Copy, description of sound effects, music, how the copy is to be delivered, TV directions, and all the elements of a radio script plus an artist's rendering of each scene—this is called a storyboard.

Each frame represents a continuation of some action, a completely new scene or an addition such as a superimposed title. Storyboards show proposed action, type and extent of locations, sets, actors, special effects and titles. A sixty-second commercial will have ten or more frames; a twenty-second commercial will have about four frames; and a ten-second commercial will have two frames. Video and audio instructions are placed under each frame.

Storyboards are developed by individuals or teams composed of the writer, a writer-artist, an artist or a writer-artist-producer.

Stick figures may be used on the storyboard and it must show proposed camera angles and focal distance. Storyboards are re-

## TELEVISION STORYBOARD

Writer's name                          Advertiser

Date                                   Product, service, appeal

Structure                              Commercial length

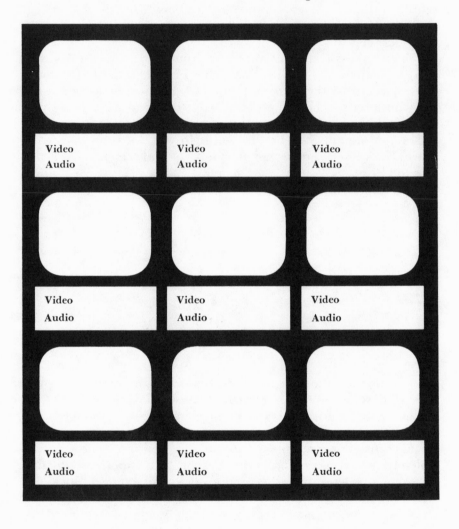

viewed by a producer who advises on sets and techniques of camera work in lab optical effects. When corrections and changes have been made, the storyboard is then sent to the agency bullpen to be drawn skillfully.

# ▪11▪ The Writer's Place in the Advertising Agency

The minimal involvement of personnel in the making of a commercial involves the following people—the client committee, usually composed of the president, vice-president, marketing director and the ad manager. The traffic department, creative director, the group head, the writer or writers, the art directors, the mechanical people, the producer, the artists, director, assistant director, the cameraman, the lighting engineers, stagehands, makeup artists, hairdressers, prop people and the film or tape editors.

All of the above is said to give you some idea of where you fit into the picture as the writer, but my job is to teach you the teachable skills of writing, and the aim of this book is to help you prepare a portfolio you can present as you go looking for that first job.

The beginning writer is often puzzled about his place in an agency. He is so absorbed in his own work that he may forget he's in the business of selling products and services with his creativity. Look at the agency organizational chart on a following page and please notice that you are in the copy department under creative services, which is superseded by account management. Your superior, the creative director, gets the order for a new campaign or a new commercial from an account executive in charge of a particular product or group of products. Without you, they can't sell effectively, but you get your direction from a creative director who gets his direction from the account executive who services a particular client. The writer always hopes the account executive has an accurate understanding of what the client really wants and has passed it along to your creative director who will give you the assignment. Often, that isn't true. That's why you may find your creative director calling you in at four in the afternoon and telling you the account executive has just returned from the client and that which you and your art director have presented as the new commercial is not what the client wants. He may also tell you that the account executive has promised the client he will re-present at ten the following morning. You know what that means. Cancel your plans. Go without dinner and stay until you've come up with an entirely new commercial. Pleasant dreams . . . once you get to bed. Set your alarm. You'll be expected back in the office at the usual time just in case the client doesn't approve the second attempt.

# AGENCY ORGANIZATIONAL CHART

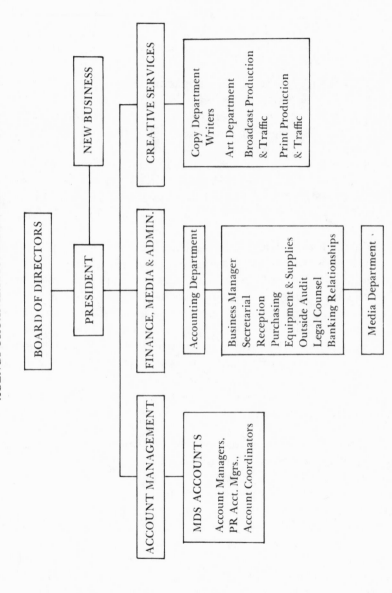

BOARD OF DIRECTORS

PRESIDENT

NEW BUSINESS

ACCOUNT MANAGEMENT

FINANCE, MEDIA & ADMIN.

CREATIVE SERVICES

**MDS ACCOUNTS**

Account Managers,
PR Acct. Mgrs.,
Account Coordinators

Accounting Department

Business Manager
Secretarial
Reception
Purchasing
Equipment & Supplies
Outside Audit
Legal Counsel
Banking Relationships

Media Department

Copy Department
Writers

Art Department

Broadcast Production
& Traffic

Print Production
& Traffic

# ▪ 12 ▪   Your Place in the TV Station

Now that you know where you stand in the organization of an agency where the commercials are written, it is important for you to have some idea of where you are in the corporate structure of a television station. The chart below will give you some idea, but there are differences according to the size of the station. As a writer, you may be a member of a certain department or "unit." Notice that the news department has its own organizational structure and writers come under reporters. If you are assigned to a certain "across-the-board" (a show seen at the same time every day, Monday through Friday) talk show, you will be in a "unit." You will have nothing to do with any other program or activity in the station. You will work on that one program. If you are not assigned to any particular show, you will get your assignments from the program director or the producer if the writing has to do with an on-air presentation.

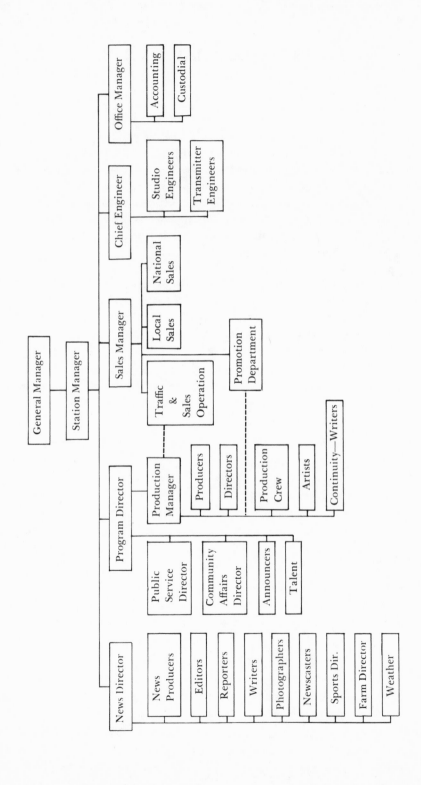

# ▪ 13 ▪    Sit Down and Start

While you will not include it in your portfolio, your first writing effort should be three hundred words on yourself. Who and what you are; what you have accomplished; what you like and your ultimate goal. Having done that you are now ready to begin the making of your portfolio.

I feel that students develop faster and learn the professional look and sound by viewing what is on television now, using their own verbal and visionary skills and watching trends. There aren't any absolute rules about anything in television. Some commercials will seem like a combination of hard and soft selling, but for our purposes we will assume that *hard sell* will mean the direct selling of a product or service and *soft sell* is the suggestive approach to the consumer.

# ▪ 14 ▪    The Hard Sell Commercial

In this technique you will mention the product many times; refer to a specific price or emphasize the words *bargain, value, savings, discount* and as many other come-ons as you can think of. You must make it clear that the consumer absolutely has to have this product; take advantage of this sale; or use this service; otherwise he is somewhat inferior or just plain stupid. Tell the consumer he just can't wait. He must act now, since most hard sell commercials are meant to produce immediate results for the advertiser.

List a half-dozen imaginary products. Choose one and WRITE A HARD SELL COMMERCIAL.

### HARD SELL

| VIDEO | AUDIO |
|---|---|
| MCU MAN STANDING IN STORE FEATURING MAJOR APPLIANCES. | CUT-EM-LOW JOE does it again. Bargains you wouldn't believe. Refrigerators 20 |

percent off; stoves sliced 30 percent; washers and dryers down 40 percent. You can't afford not to take advantage of these prices right now. Stereos and color television sets at prices you can afford. All the famous brand names. Are you gonna wait until the prices go up? Never again will CUT-EM-LOW JOE have such great bargains. You have to come right now.

Cash-and-carry only or arrange your own delivery. There's something for everybody. Will you be the only one on your block without a dishwasher? 40 percent off right now at CUT-EM-LOW JOE's special sale on every appliance in the store. Don't wait for that dream to come true. Don't put off what you can have today. Hurry on down right now. Finish your home today. Don't wait. CUT-EM-LOW JOE isn't making money. He's saving it for you. CUT-EM-LOW JOE. NOW!

### Analysis

A perfect example of the low-cost commercial with a pitchman who is covering a whole store. The appeal is to the low- and middle-income viewer who wants and perhaps needs the very items he mentions. Urgency is the key word. "Are you gonna wait until the prices go up?" "You have to come right now." "Hurry." All of this is emphasized with an appeal to vanity, the need "to belong" ... that is, "Will you be the only one on your block without a dishwasher?" That might be just the phrase that will catch the ear of the woman who watches her neighbor take off in the second car and leave the dishwasher running while she stands in the window scrubbing away. Instant gratification and realization is touched upon and finally "CUT-EM-LOW JOE" is saving you money and doing you a big favor. Sure he is.

   Don't laugh. Some clients want just this kind of commercial and when the salesman comes back with the order in his pocket you have to come through. Grit your teeth and plunge in with the full gamut of emotional appeals in your copy.

## HARD SELL

| VIDEO | AUDIO |
|---|---|
| MLS SHOE SALESMAN REPLACING SHOE ON CUSTOMER. CUSTOMER STANDS AND WALKS OUT OF FRAME TO ENTRANCE WITH SALESMAN IN BACKGROUND. | |
| DOLLY IN MCU SHOE SALESMAN. | That guy needs ENDODORS. In this job, I meet a lot of well-dressed people with smelly feet. I tell them about ENDODORS, but they don't always take the hint. |
| CUT TO ECU ENDODORS AS A HAND SLIPS THEM INTO A SHOE. | ENDODORS are innersoles treated with charcoal to absorb odors and perspiration. You don't have to take off your shoes for other people to smell your feet. Are you sure you don't need ENDODORS? Make sure. Buy ENDODORS today. Keep your feet smelling sweet. ENDODORS makes it a lot easier on you, your friends . . . and me. |
| MCU SHOE SALESMAN. | |
| MCU SALESMAN WITH PACKAGE OF ENDODORS. | ENDODORS. |

### *Analysis*

   This commercial is slightly lower key, but it's still hard sell. I can guarantee you that every viewer who sees it will smell his shoes before putting in the shoetrees and will probably buy the product if he detects the slightest odor. The product name is repeated over and over. It will never be forgotten. A self-consciousness has been created about a problem many people have. The spokesperson creates sympathy for the friends and business associates of the viewer. Look for everyday situations to which you can relate your product. In this instance, you've touched upon a need and a delicate problem. Exploit it. Create doubt. Make the viewer think about a problem he may not have, but urge him to take precautions by buying your product. You are solving a problem for some, arousing awareness for others and you are selling everyone.

# ▪ 15 ▪ The Soft Sell Commercial

This kind of commercial is persuasive and easier on the ears than the hard sell commercial, which is usually delivered with rapid speech and perhaps much volume.

Remember that the basic needs of human beings are health, housing, food, clothing, acceptance, recognition and pride. Focus your commercial on the human emotions of security, vanity, pleasure, daring and value. Remember that people react from instinct: fear, personal goals, envy of others, the need to "belong" as well as feelings of self-esteem and nostalgia.

WRITE A SOFT SELL COMMERCIAL. USE A DIFFERENT TIME LENGTH.

## SOFT SELL

| VIDEO | AUDIO |
|---|---|
| MCU WOMAN IN LATE TWENTIES OR EARLY THIRTIES. | Women have very special needs. A nutritious diet is not enough without an iron supplement. We lose a lot of iron and unless we replace it every day we can experience a loss of strength and vitality. We all need SUP-IRON. A tiny tablet |
| SUPER SUP-IRON | of SUP-IRON taken every day keeps your iron level just where it should be. Minerals are a woman's best friend. SUP-IRON—every day—for you. |

## *Analysis*

The commercial is shorter. We will get into timing later. Right now, I'm trying to loosen you up and let you roll. We can "trim" later. You are writing freely. Saying what you have to say and some of what you want to say. Enjoy this liberty. It doesn't last.

This soft sell commercial concerns a little recognized health problem and speaks of it with dignity and restraint. It calls attention to a common complaint—"loss of strength and vitality"—and offers a simple solution. Restraint and understatement are the key words in the soft sell commercial and they can be applied to almost any product or service. You match your style with the image of the advertiser or you create an image for the advertiser with the style of your commercial. It all depends on how the advertiser sees himself and how successful the salesman is in making the advertiser view his product or service realistically. Most advertisers know what they want and what they are doing. An advertiser who appeals to low- and middle-income consumers may want a "class" image as he rises on the economic scale. This is wrong for him, but it's not your job to tell him so. Your job is to take your direction from your creative director and the account executive in the agency or the salesperson in the station. It often humbles one.

## SOFT SELL

| VIDEO | AUDIO |
|---|---|
| SLIDE #1 COTTON FIELD CUT TO MCU MOTHER ENFOLDING BABY IN THICK TOWEL. | MUSIC: UP AND UNDER ANNCR VO Cotton. It's soft. Naturally. |
| SLIDE #2 COTTON COUNCIL OF AMERICA | MUSIC: OUT |

## *Analysis*

With ever-increasing costs of production and television time, the ten-second commercial is becoming more and more popular. Here you've said it all. Nature. Mother. Baby. Product. Benefit. The least said the better . . . *ALWAYS* . . . in a soft sell commercial. They are challenging to write and very satisfying when effectively produced with appealing video.

# ▪ 16 ▪  The Situation Commercial

You are now ready to tackle your first commercial for television.
Remember that writing is the exploration and selection of ideas,
visualization of persons and situations, and the joining of words.

In your first television commerical, begin with a situation commerical. The situation commercial tells a story. It must have a
simple plot and be easy to follow. Establish a reason for the exis-
tence of the product and keep in mind that almost all commercials
are based on three steps—problem, solution and result.

Your commercial must have an eye-and-ear-arresting beginning,
an explanatory middle and an ending that promises satisfaction.
Viewers must follow this sequence and become involved. Your
motives as a writer are to attract attention and arouse emotion—
a longing; remembered experience; the resolution of a frustration;
the creation of suspense. Build to a climax and end with a believable and satisfying solution.

The commercial should tell how to look better, feel better, protect or improve health and life, experience sensual beauty or social
acceptance or feel more secure.

If the viewer believes what he sees and hears, he'll probably buy
the product with the expectancy of realizing the promise of your
product.

Develop your situation carefully. Each step in the story must
relate to and follow the point that has gone before. Can your
commercial be followed easily? Have you developed your commercial in a logical and believable sequence?

Pace is all important. Be sure your viewer understands everything you say point to point. Hold his attention and build to the
finale.

1.  Have a plot.
2.  Keep it simple.
3.  Develop the plot one step at a time.
4.  Be believable.
5.  Check your beginning to see if it arrests the viewer's attention immediately.
6.  Identify the situation.
7.  Mention the product.

8.   Define the performance of the product.

9.   Relate product performance to satisfaction.

10.   Urge the viewer to buy the product with an action verb: *get, buy, ask for,* etc.

Emphasize the name of the product.
WRITE A TELEVISION SITUATION COMMERCIAL.

## SITUATION COMMERCIAL

| VIDEO | AUDIO |
|---|---|
| MCU MAN AND WOMAN SITTING AT BREAKFAST TABLE LADEN WITH FOOD. MAN SIPS COFFEE; GETS UP TO LEAVE. | |
| | **MAN**<br>Gotta run. I'll miss my train. |
| | **WOMAN**<br>Tom, you do this every morning. I get up at five-thirty to make breakfast and you never eat. |
| WOMAN RISES FROM TABLE. | **MAN**<br>I've told you not to. It's a ninety-minute commute if I'm lucky and I don't have time. See you after seven. |
| MAN LEAVES WITH WOMAN STARING AFTER HIM. CUT TO MCU WOMAN IN SUPERMARKET EXAMINING PACKAGE. | **WOMAN**<br>(*Reads*)<br>EARLY BIRD Breakfast Bars. Two EARLY BIRD Breakfast Bars with a glass of milk are as nourishing as a bacon-and-egg breakfast. All the vitamins and minerals of the usual breakfast. That's it. |

| | |
|---|---|
| DISSOLVE TO MAN AT HOME AT BREAKFAST TABLE WITH PACKAGE OF EARLY BIRD BREAKFAST BARS AND PITCHER OF MILK. | MAN<br>My wife's sleeping in. She gets her rest and I get breakfast with EARLY BIRD Breakfast Bars and a glass of milk. Yesterday—apple, today—raisin, and tomorrow—maple flavor. I get the nourishment I need to start the day. She feels better and I wouldn't tell her, but so do I. EARLY BIRD Breakfast Bars. A good solid breakfast. Try 'em. |
| (MAN WINKS) | |
| (MAN PICKS UP PACKAGE) | |

## SITUATION COMMERCIAL

| VIDEO | AUDIO |
|---|---|
| MCU MAN DRESSED FOR WORK STANDING AT BREAKFAST TABLE. | MAN<br>I used to skip breakfast and then my wife complained I didn't eat right. She'd get up and fix a meal, but I didn't have time and then she'd feel hurt and I'd feel guilty. |
| CUT TO PACKAGE OF EARLY BIRD BREAKFAST BARS AND PITCHER OF MILK. | Then I heard about EARLY BIRD Breakfast Bars. They come in different flavors and with a glass of milk, I feel as |
| ECU THREE PACKAGES OF EB BREAKFAST BARS. | though I've had breakfast. I really haven't, you know, but it tastes good and that's what counts. Besides, my wife's |
| CUT TO ECU MAN TAKING A BITE AND CHEWING. | satisfied now. You try 'em and you'll see. |

### *Analysis*

What is the difference between the first situation commercial and the second? In number one, we establish a situation with much conflict, a genuine need, an attempt to resolve the conflict of a man who has little time and a woman who'd rather sleep but feels a sense of duty and finally resolves everything with a product. The nutritive value is clearly defined; the variety of taste appeal is mentioned with enthusiasm and the spokesman shares his total satisfaction with us.

In the second commercial, we start out with a negative situation. The man doesn't take care of his health; he presents his wife as a shrew and he takes credit for finding the answer. If he's that busy, he won't be on the alert for a breakfast food. The taste appeal is not defined and the nutritional value is ignored. The entire commercial and sale of the product is negated when he says he really hasn't eaten breakfast but "it tastes good." He ignores the benefit to himself and speaks only about being relieved of his wife's complaints. Most of all, the name of the product is mentioned only once. He isn't really sold and you won't be either. Such commercials are still written and are used when the spokesperson is well known and the advertiser mistakenly thinks a familiar face can be translated into familiarity with his product. Notice the sparse video. The commercial ends with a man chewing (probably with his mouth open) rather than a shot of the product.

# ▪ 17 ▪ Promises, Promises

The "promises" commercial is a problem-solving commercial. Identify the problem. Establish a relationship between the problem and the viewer; demonstrate the product; list the product benefits (POS—points of sale) and end by mentioning the rewards of using the product.

The promise commercial is more acceptable if the product has qualities that can be stated simply and demonstrated. If the problem seems exaggerated or unimportant to the viewer, he or she is likely to feel ridiculous. More importantly, the viewer will probably react negatively to the product you are trying to sell.

The solution of the problem must be presented in a believable way without artificiality or telegraphed predictability. Avoid authoritarian or technical explanations. Simple declarative sentences preclude the gush of exaggerated enthusiasm.

Develop the commercial by stating a problem that the viewer has heard about, experienced or wants to avoid. If the viewer understands what you are saying and you don't overcolor the problem, the viewer will believe you.

Dramatize the qualities of the product in the demonstration and mention only those claims that are pertinent to the problem. Don't clutter the commercial with too many people or too many words. If the viewer believes the person on the screen knows and understands what he is talking about, he will believe in the product.

Introduce the product in a natural, even ordinary way and immediately hold out the possibility of a solution to the problem.

Too many genies, warlocks, convenient friends and off-camera announcers are used in commercial introductions.

All you have to do is introduce the product, explain the usage and benefits of the product, state and demonstrate the solution and let the viewer decide what reward to expect.

If you haven't exaggerated, you've given consumer service not puffery.

Emphasize the name of the product.

WRITE A TELEVISION COMMERCIAL THAT MAKES A PROMISE.

## PROMISES, PROMISES #1

| VIDEO | AUDIO |
|---|---|
| MLS SHAMPOO ROOM OF BEAUTY SALON. CAMERA ZOOMS IN TO ONE BASIN. CUSTOMER SITS IN CHAIR, SHAMPOO GIRL IS RINSING. POMERANIAN SITS ON CUSTOMER'S LAP. | SHAMPOO GIRL<br>Oh, no. Not again.<br><br>CUSTOMER<br>Is there a problem?<br><br>SHAMPOO GIRL<br>Same old thing. Hair clogs in the drain.<br><br>CUSTOMER<br>You should try CLEARUP.<br>Frances uses it all the time in |

my apartment. She says it's the one drain cleaner that actually dissolves hair, grease and detergent scum. I know she's right. I bathe Poopy Baby right in the lavatory and she does lose some hair, but with CLEARUP, my drains always flow fast and freely.

DOLLY IN ECU ON DOG, POOPY BABY.

DISSOLVE TO MCU CUSTOMER DRESSED AND COIFFED. HANDS TIP TO SHAMPOO GIRL.

SHAMPOO GIRL
I'll send down for some.

CUSTOMER
Here's your tip and thank you.

SHAMPOO GIRL
That's two tips. The best one was finding out about CLEARUP, the new drain cleaner that actually dissolves everything . . . even hair. Thank you.

CUSTOMER
Thank Poopy Baby. If it weren't for her, Frances and I would never have known about CLEARUP.

SHAMPOO GIRL
Thank you, Poopy Baby.

CUSTOMER
See you next week.
    (To dog)
Come with Mama.

CUSTOMER WALKS AWAY WITH DOG.

MCU SHAMPOO GIRL.

SHAMPOO GIRL HOLDS UP CAN OF CLEARUP.

SHAMPOO GIRL
Mama knows best . . . at least about drain cleaners. CLEARUP—the drain cleaner that dissolves everything in your drain.

## PROMISES, PROMISES #2

| VIDEO | AUDIO |
|---|---|
| MCU PLUMBER WITH CAN OF CLEARUP. | **PLUMBER**<br>All day long I get calls. Usually nothing but a stopped-up drain. I can't make any money that way. With **CLEARUP** I can just pour half a cup of grains down the drain and in ten minutes, the clog is gone. **CLEARUP** outclogs all other cleaners. Get some today. Don't call me. Call for |
| ECU CAN OF CLEARUP. | **CLEARUP**. |

### *Analysis*

The first "Promise" commercial is specific about the kinds of accumulations that are solved by the product. The setting for the action is familiar to women and they associate themselves immediately with the product. They are buoyed with the expectancy of being able to handle the problem inexpensively and they are entertained by the paradox of an affluent woman with knowledge of a product like a drain cleaner. Women viewers will believe this commercial.

The second "Promise" commercial is the usual stand-up pitch. The sight of a professional plumber doesn't add to the believability of the product and the copy is likely to make women feel dependent and stupid. In this and future eras, women are and will be eager to do things for themselves. They want to know exactly what a product will do before they spend the money, and it is they who do most of the buying.

Can you improve upon the first "Promise" commercial? There is a way and I hope you will.

All of the "sample" commercials are the merest suggestion of how a commercial should read to cover the points made in the rules of structure. You can write "finished" commercials and that's what I'm trying to encourage you to do.

# ▪ 18 ▪ The Sequential Commercial

The sequential television commercial is usually the creation of the art director. It is used to demonstrate development, emphasize status, diversity and stability. Minimum copy and captivating visuals tell the sales story, supported by emotional appeal. Camera work and lighting create tone and ambiance.

It is important to "plot" a sequential commercial. The preparation is not unlike writing a recipe. The successive incidents flowing from one into another are the "ingredients" of your sequential commercial.

Ask yourself some questions.

1.  How was the product developed?

Or in the instance of an institutional sequential commercial,

2.  How did the business begin?

3.  What is the product or institutional image?

4.  What standards are maintained?

5.  What improvements have been made?

6.  Am I trying to elicit a recall of an experience?

7.  Am I appealing to an experience the viewer would like to realize?

8.  What emotion am I trying to arouse?

Write an outline of the nonfictional story you want to tell. Visualize! Visualize! Visualize!

See each scene merging into the next scene and you won't need many words. If possible, use a voice over and avoid the distraction of a personality. The pictures are the storyteller.

If you must indicate a lapse of time, do so gently with a wipe (a control technique where one picture is replaced by another and the new picture crowds off the first by pushing it off to one side, to the top or to the bottom) or dissolve (one shot dissolves into a new one). If you need time for your conclusion, don't be afraid of abrupt cuts.

Believable development with an outcome of satisfaction or at least a reassuring promise is your goal.

Emphasize the name of the product.

WRITE A SEQUENTIAL TELEVISION COMMERCIAL.

# SEQUENTIAL

| VIDEO | AUDIO |
|-------|-------|
| SFX | ANNCR VO |
| STOCK FILM OF ERA. | At the turn of the century when love was romantic with a touch of elegance, WINDSOR HOUSE was a small jewelry store. Men came to buy bracelets for their daughter, lockets for their sweetheart and a wedding ring for their bride-to-be. |
| SLIDE #1 | |
| CUT TO JEWELRY DISPLAY. | |
| WIPE TO TWENTIES COUPLE. | Later, we added jeweled cigarette holders for the flappers and silver flasks for young men who knew someone at a speakeasy. We kept expanding in size and in our awareness that people came to WINDSOR HOUSE for quality. We offered the finest in silver and china from all over the world and later we built a new building to include everything needed for the good life, all of the time for some, and those special highlights of life for many. |
| DISSOLVE TO DISPLAY OF FINE SILVER AND CHINA. | |
| FILM—PRESENT BUILDING. | |
| CUT TO INTERIOR OF BUILDING. PAN TABLE OF CONTENTS. | Today, we house the largest collection of precious jewels, gold, silver, china, crystal, linen, stationery and objets d'art in the country. Some people come just to look, and you're welcome . . . because we know when you want the best, you'll buy at |
| SLIDE LOGO | WINDSOR HOUSE. |

# SEQUENTIAL

| VIDEO | AUDIO |
|---|---|
| SFX | ANNCR VO |
| FADE IN INT. OF BUILDING. | At WINDSOR HOUSE we are |
| PAN COUNTERS. | the servants of those with taste. |
| | People of breeding who have |
| | always known the good life and |
| | appreciate the finest in jewelry, |
| | china, gold, silver, linens and |
| | objets d'art. Quality has always |
| | been the key word at |
| | WINDSOR HOUSE. From the |
| SLIDE #1 | very beginning, our clientele |
| | has been the *crème de la crème* of |
| | society. For every occasion— |
| QUICK CUTS OF ELEGANT | birthdays, graduations, |
| CELEBRATIONS. | anniversaries, weddings and |
| | any day you feel the urge to |
| | give only the best—WINDSOR |
| | HOUSE has been there for |
| | those who know. Our exclusive |
| | registry service enables all our |
| | customers to make every day |
| | memorable for some one. For |
| | the best people . . . the best is |
| SLIDE LOGO | at WINDSOR HOUSE. |

## *Analysis*

The first sequential commercial has a beginning, middle and an end. It has continuity, warmth, nostalgia and appeal to all people. The image of quality and security is maintained with the mere hint of status. A goal, something to which to aspire, has been preserved without offense to or exclusion of anyone. It develops slowly and shows diversity of service; a story of growth without sacrificing standards and a recognition of the dignity of all persons.

I hope I don't have to tell you what's wrong with the second sequential commercial. People who are regular customers of a store like this don't need to be told that it's there to meet their needs and desires. This second commercial is sheer snobbery. Arrogant. Exclusive. Disdainful. This commercial will not even increase store traffic, much less profit. Television is a mass media and the money of the masses is just as green as that of the "best people." If you are going to write a sequential commercial showing the growth and development of an institution, include your viewers—don't put up the "red rope" that excludes anyone.

The sequential commercial is ideal for demonstrating how a car is built and the newest features of the latest models; how a wine is made; or the step-by-step manufacture of a product. If you know about any one of these things, try a sequential commercial on one of them. BE SURE YOU KNOW. You must follow sequence and the less said, the better. I happen to be fascinated by diversification in a business as long as the parts are related. I know about this and I chose to write a sequential commercial about something I know and appreciate. If I had an assignment about something I didn't know about, I should have to spend hours in research. It can be done, but remember there are copy specialists who write exclusively about cars, wine, bread, beer and cosmetics. Unfortunately, we seldom see a sequential commercial. Writers describe a process in the making of a product because that's their direction, but some clients are aware of the value of pictures with a few words. This is the ideal commercial structure on which to test your ability to visualize.

The best direction I can give you is to think of a recipe. . . . Start with this ingredient, add a cup of that ingredient, put in a quarter teaspoon of something else and so on until the finished product is seen. You could write a commercial about a frozen food or a fast-food specialty (one fast-food chain does it very well—first the meat, then the tomato, cheese, onions, sauce, and so forth, and voilà. . . . their latest concoction), but the sequence must be there. The sequential commercial done well with detailed visuals is as close to an art form as television can get. Presently, I don't see one on the air as a good example. The trend of today is a fast ten or twenty seconds of "Here's the product [category]; this is the name of the product; this is what it does; go out and buy it." It bothers me that there is such a sameness about most commercials. Few are entertaining or give an incentive to buy. Change that. You can.

# ▪ 19 ▪  In the Mood

Special effects are used to tell the atmospheric or mood commercial. Camera effects must flow unobtrusively, but you can use a great variety of them.

You are not making promises, giving problem solutions or telling a story in this kind of commercial. You are creating a mood that identifies with the product and what it does. In the mood commercial you must be very careful that the features of the product and, above all, the NAME of the product are not overshadowed by camera techniques, music or a beautiful or exotic setting.

At a 1978 Christmas party, eleven adults oohed and aahed over a beer commercial, but there were three different opinions about which beer it was! With this commercial, it is easy to gain viewers but lose sales.

Make the mood commercial memorable only in the sense of giving a product a personality of its own.

Emphasize the name of the product.

WRITE A MOOD TELEVISION COMMERCIAL.

| VIDEO | AUDIO |
|---|---|
| SFX | MUSIC: DELICATE—UP AND UNDER |
| MLS GIRL IN EVENING DRESS AT MUSEUM EXHIBITION. | ANNCR VO<br>Out of the splendor of the Orient; an echo of the ancient East with the touch of this moment in time. |
| ZOOM IN MCU GIRL. | PERSIAN MELON . . . a rich golden tone with undertones of coral. |
| ECU GIRL TOUCHES CHEEK. | PERSIAN MELON, for your lips or fingertips. Lipstick rich with moisturizers; and nail polish . . . thick . . . smooth. |
| DOLLY OUT FOR MLS GIRL. | PERSIAN MELON from Lorane . . . for all your magic moments.<br>MUSIC: OUT |

### Analysis

We have created a mood to go with the name of the new shade of lipstick and nail polish that our client is introducing. Much depends on the set, lighting, choice of music, movement of the model and the quality of the voice of the announcer. Tempo is the key word for all of this and the key words for you, the writer, are:

1.   Set the scene with words related to the product.
2.   Mention the product.
3.   Talk about the characteristics of the product.
4.   Let the video carry the mood.
5.   Stop before you break the mood.

The mood commercial is often used with cosmetic commercials. Every commercial has "flavor," but the mood commercial must arouse a certain emotion equated with the product.


# ▪20▪          Say It's So


Many advertisers feel that the word of mouth or testimonial commercial is the most effective. They think that viewers are likely to buy a product or service or respond to an appeal if they admire the person giving the testimonial or identify with the personality. A well-known figure or an unknown person may be the central figure, but the special appeal of this kind of commercial is that the product is attested to and recommended by a person. Equally important is the message and the viewer. If the person performing the commercial is well known, there is an advantage sometimes, but there is often the risk of a disadvantage. The well-known person may capture the attention of the viewer, but it's possible that interest and pleasure in seeing the celebrity will diminish or even eclipse the message and maybe obscure the name of the product. It is not unusual for a viewer to mention seeing a favorite actor "doing" a commercial, but if you ask what he was selling, most viewers don't remember. The product is of first importance.

Celebrities cost a lot of money and the writer must be as conscious of costs as anyone else. Usually, a product can be sold just as effectively with an unknown. All you need is someone who can make you believe that he or she believes in the product, uses it and finds it beneficial. An unknown person can testify to a product because of the ego satisfaction involved. If an unknown seems natural and sincere, you have the necessary believability and persuasion. When we speak of an "unknown person" we mean a trained actor or actress. Some advertisers talk about and practice the use of what they call "real" people. Actors and actresses are "real" people too. The truly professional advertiser is not going to increase his production costs by using nonprofessionals who require hours of instruction and are paid the same amount of money that would be earned by an actor or actress who has spent time and money training for television performance. These "real" people are one-shots who take jobs away from people who are qualified and are just as believable. Certainly, professionals speak more clearly and are much more at ease before the camera.

One advertising agency that was committed to the use of "real" people will no longer hire anyone but a professional actor or actress. This agency learned a lesson that ended in tragedy when it hired a group of housewives to perform in a commercial for a cleaning product. The ladies were brought into the city from the suburbs and small towns, wined, dined, coiffed, taken on sight-seeing trips and rehearsed and rehearsed. One of the "real" ladies returned to her home after the commercial was taped and reentered her world of clamoring children, a devoted if unglamorous husband, and a life of cleaning and cooking. The euphoria of her big moment lasted until the commercial was aired. She telephoned the agency repeatedly for an opportunity to make another commercial and learned they had no further interest in her. Her dreams of a new life and fame and fortune were shattered. She hanged herself. The agency and the client were shocked and filled with guilt, and a firm policy designating professionals only was established that day and has been followed ever since.

While that incident may seem extreme, it certainly makes a case for the professional performer who knows that he lives in a world of rejection where on the average he will get one job out of twenty-five auditions—if he's lucky and very competent.

Some basic rules for the writing of the believable commercial are:

1.  Your viewers must believe that the person giving the sales pitch is someone who is likely to use the product. A well-known seductive actress would hardly be convincing as the spokeswoman for an oven cleaner.

2.  Try to meet the commercial performer who will speak your words. Listen to the pace, rhythm and tonality of the voice and make any necessary changes. Observe eye movement and ges-

tures and try to write for that person. It saves production time and costs if the performer is comfortable with the material.

3.   Don't use a person who appears in too many commercials or is identified with another product. "Mr. Whipple" knows that he's stuck with a certain toilet paper for the rest of his professional life.

4.   If you can find an expert in a profession that relates to your product, use that person. Jimmy Connors would be believed as a seller of tennis equipment.

Avoid gimmicks. Simple sets and a straightforward message with minimum movement give focus to the product and assure credibility.

WRITE A "BELIEVABLE" TELEVISION COMMERCIAL.

## SAY IT'S SO

| VIDEO | AUDIO |
|---|---|
| MLS BASKETBALL COURT. | (SFX CROWD AND REFEREE WHISTLE AT BASKETBALL GAME) |
| MCU ERNIE COATES. | Hi. I'm Ernie Coates. When I'm on the court, I don't want to have to think about anything but the game. RESIL basketball shoes give me the confidence I need. RESIL is not just an |
| CUT TO ECU OF INNER CONSTRUCTION OF SHOE. | ordinary sneaker. Strong, ankle-snug canvas tops and thick multilayered soles of rubber, cushioned with foam between the rubber layers, give me the bounce for a jump and the stability for a fast pivot I |
| MCU ERNIE COATES. | need. RESIL shoes are the best. On the basketball or tennis court, for jogging or to wear on your boat . . . RESIL shoes give you comfort and flexibility. RESIL shoes cost a little more . . . but I'd rather pay more and have fleet feet than turn an ankle or lose a game. Get RESIL shoes . . . the sportsman's favorite. |

# SAY IT'S SO

| VIDEO | AUDIO |
|---|---|
| MCU ERNIE COATES. | Hi, I'm Ernie Coates. When I'm not on the court playing basketball, I like to fool around in the kitchen. But with DYNARANGE, there's no fooling around. I just pick up what I want to eat, put it in my DYNARANGE; set the timer and within minutes I've got myself a meal. No overcooking or undercooking. Just perfect every time. Get yourself a DYNARANGE and score every time. DYNARANGE . . . it makes cooking a pleasure. |

## *Analysis*

In the first example, we've taken a "famous" sports figure and given him something to talk about with which he is familiar. The special features of the "product" are well defined and shown, and the benefits of spending more money for a shoe are made very clear and related to other sports as well. This commercial will be believed. Your spokesperson could be an unknown actor portraying a shoe salesman who sells to sports figures. In either case, the "product" will be remembered.

In the second commercial, the prominent athlete is talking about something with which he cannot be identified easily. He hasn't told us anything about the features of the product and women viewers will want to know about that before spending money. This commercial lacks spokesperson-product identity or spokesperson-viewer relationship, and we know nothing about how this appliance works or is made. This is the kind of commercial often done to put some green stuff into the pockets of a well-known person. Kids will yell, "Hey, Mom, Ernie Coates is on," without caring about what he says. We can only hope that no Ernie Coates fan will go out and buy a DYNARANGE and bring it home to his wife when she knows another product is more reliable. Be a matchmaker with celebrities and products.

# ▪ 21 ▪   We're Only Human

The human situation has often been thought about as satirical and the satire structure in a television commercial is as difficult as life itself can sometimes be. Writers like satire but few do it well.

True satire is not bitter or cutting but rather good-natured observation of human folly, absurd situations, eccentric characters, ridiculous events or public figures who have distinctive mannerisms or habits. Satire is always an exaggeration and must be presented as such. Overexaggeration becomes slapstick and the shared fun is lost.

The person, event or situation must be familiar to the viewer, and the visuals, commentary and imitations must be presented with a light touch. Viewers enjoy satire in small doses as long as it makes a point, but it can become tiresome very quickly. Overdone or prolonged satire can hurt the sale of your product. Ask yourself:

1.  Will viewers know the subject?
2.  Will viewers know this is a lampoon?
3.  Am I hurting anyone?
4.  Am I offending anyone?
5.  Is the viewer laughing with me or AT someone or something?
6.  Am I joking or condemning?
7.  Does the point of sale offer a solution after the satirization?

Emphasize the name of your product.
WRITE A SATIRICAL TELEVISION COMMERCIAL.

Writing satire is one of the most difficult of all assignments. Many writers steer away from it completely and some very funny satire is rejected because the television audience is made up of so many different ethnic groups, political preferences and persons who have been stereotyped by the media or generational pass-alongs. Here are some subjects to avoid:

Mothers-in-law                  Ethnic figures
Elderly people                  Ethnic groups
Political figures               Minorities

All of these subjects have been used and abused in lame attempts at satire and all have created controversy. Stand-up comics and some talk-show hosts can get away with mild references to some of the categories mentioned above, but someone is always hurt or embarrassed despite the encouragement and laughter of the spectators. You are selling a product or service, and if you alienate even a small part of your viewing audience, you have hurt sales for the man who is paying the bills.

## WE'RE ONLY HUMAN

| VIDEO | AUDIO |
|---|---|
| MLS BEWILDERED CUSTOMER COMES IN DOOR AND BANK OFFICER APPROACHES. | **BANK OFFICER**<br>May I help you?<br><br>**CUSTOMER**<br>No, thank you . . . I was looking for the MUTUAL BANK.<br>**BANK OFFICER**<br>This *is* the MUTUAL BANK. |
| LS BANK INTERIOR. PAN DISPLAY OF GIFTS. | **CUSTOMER**<br>This is a bank? Blankets, toasters, stereos and golf clubs?<br><br>**BANK OFFICER**<br>Oh, yes. These are the gifts we give our customers for opening a checking account with interest. |
| MLS CUSTOMER AND BANK OFFICER. | **CUSTOMER**<br>You mean savings.<br><br>**BANK OFFICER**<br>I mean checking.<br><br>**CUSTOMER**<br>What's the catch?<br><br>**BANK OFFICER**<br>No catch . . . except the gifts. At MUTUAL BANK you can open a checking account with interest with a deposit of from one to five thousand dollars. |

|  |  |
|---|---|
|  | **CUSTOMER**<br>One to five thousand dollars. |
| TRACK CUSTOMER AND<br>BANK OFFICER. | **BANK OFFICER**<br>That's right. Now step right over here and I'll show you how to earn interest on a checking account. |
|  | **CUSTOMER**<br>*(Voice trailing)*<br>About those golf clubs . . . how much? . . . |
| CUT TO BANK LOGO | **ANNCR VO**<br>Go to your MUTUAL BANK today. Find out how you can earn money on your checking account. MUTUAL BANK is your money-maker. |

## WE'RE ONLY HUMAN

| VIDEO | AUDIO |
|---|---|
| MLS COMFORTABLY CROWDED BAR. WELL-DRESSED MAN ENTERS AND SITS AT BAR. | **BARTENDER**<br>*(Faking accent)*<br>Ah, if it isn't Patrick O'Day himself . . . all dressed up in his Sunday-go-to-meetin' clothes. And where might you be goin'? |
| MCU BARTENDER AND CUSTOMER. | **PATRICK**<br>I missed my train. I'm on my way home. |
|  | **BARTENDER**<br>Ya mean ya been at work? . . . Well have a draft or better yet a boilermaker. |

PATRICK

No thanks. I'll have a glass of HORST white wine.

BARTENDER

HORST white wine? Now is that a drink for an Irishman? Come on, you may be a lawyer, but everybody knows the Irish. Have a good double belt and mix it up like a true lad of the old sod.

PATRICK

A glass of HORST white wine, please.

BARTENDER

*(Mocking)*

HORST White wine, please.

PATRICK

Excuse me.

MCU PATRICK LEAVES BAR
AND ANOTHER CUSTOMER
TAKES HIS SEAT.

BARTENDER

Hey, wait a minute. I got it. Now why would he leave and why would an Irishman want a glass of white wine?

CUSTOMER AT BAR

Because—HORST white wine is for everyone. It's gentle, refreshing with a dry, cooling taste.

SECOND CUSTOMER

HORST white wine. That's what I'm having. How about you?

MCU SECOND CUSTOMER
FACING CAMERA.

SECOND CUSTOMER VO

HORST white wine . . . for easy refreshment.

ECU BOTTLE OF HORST
WHITE WINE.

### Analysis

Our first commercial is an easily identifiable situation with a message of service and advantage. There is good-natured fun poked at banks and their "gifts," but a definite "selling" point is made and viewers will likely go into a bank to ask questions if nothing else. Information, good will and what seems like "something for nothing" is offered and presented much more graphically than could be done in print.

The flaws in the second commercial are so obvious we hardly need to list them. An ethnic slur and a sweeping generalization about a stereotype is given by the main character. One sale is lost and it is merely suggested that another is to be made. Viewers of a certain lineage will NEVER buy this wine and thinking viewers will avoid it.

You can take this same situation and product and write an inoffensive commercial which promotes sales. Think and try.

## ▪ 22 ▪     Show and Tell

Show and tell commercials demonstrate a product's ability to give greater satisfaction than a competitive product.

The essence of this commercial is to prove that a product does what you say it will do. The first five seconds are of the utmost importance. Catch the viewer's attention at the opening and keep it all the way through. Demonstrate product performance with total honesty. Does the commercial inspire confidence? Have you made the viewer feel that he can try the product and prove the claims you have made are true?

Keep your demonstration honest. The show and tell commercial is not a sleight-of-hand performance. Keep the camera on the demonstration from start to finish and don't try tricks. Encourage the interest of the viewer with close-ups. Your viewer and potential buyer of the product deserves the privilege of as much examination as the camera can produce.

Don't clutter the audio with a lot of technical jargon. The manufacturer of the product may be very proud of a technical feature, but your viewer just wants to know if it works. Try the demonstration yourself. If you're convinced, you'll write convincingly.

1.  Tell your viewer what you are going to do.
2.  Explain what you want to prove.
3.  Show your viewer what happens when you do it.

4.  Show the proof.

In this commercial, you write more video and less audio.
Emphasize the name of the product.
WRITE A SHOW AND TELL COMMERCIAL.

## SHOW AND TELL

| VIDEO | AUDIO |
|---|---|
| MCU WOMAN STANDING BEHIND BUTCHER BLOCK WITH CHOPMIX APPLIANCE. | My kitchen looked like the appliance department of a store. This gadget. That gadget, and no place to store anything. I want to show you how one appliance . . . |
| ECU MACHINE CHOPS BEEF AND FINGER TOUCHES SWITCH. ECU COFFEE GRINDING. ECU TOMATO AND CUCUMBER SLICES FALL INTO NEAT PILES. | CHOPMIX . . . does all your precooking chores. CHOPMIX grinds meat . . . flip a switch— grinds coffee . . . flip a switch— slices tomatoes or cucumbers . . . |
| ECU HAND INSERTING HALF AN ORANGE. ECU APPLE BEING DICED. ECU FRUIT AND JUICE SLIDING DOWN FUNNEL INTO BLENDER ATTACHMENT. | Extracts fruit juice . . . Dices fruit and with another flip, the fruit or vegetables or juice slide gently into the blender. |
| ECU BLENDER IN MOTION WITH INGREDIENTS WHIPPING AROUND. | |
| MCU WOMAN WITH HAND RESTING ON MOTIONLESS APPLIANCE. | Push a button . . . And whirl away with CHOPMIX. CHOPMIX . . . the one appliance for food preparation. All you do is flip and push and CHOPMIX does the rest. CHOPMIX in your favorite store. |

## Analysis

We've told the viewer about a time- and trouble-saving device.
We've explained what we are going to do.
We demonstrate all the uses of the product.
We proved the genius of this product.

The copy could be shortened just by naming the ingredients that the machine can handle, but we aren't ready to talk about commercial length until you are first conversant with various structures.


# ▪ 23 ▪    Will It or Won't It?


A "will it or won't it" commercial is built on suspense.

The difference between this and other commercials is that you are establishing inquisitive interest, creating a conflict between hope and doubt, maintaining a "wait and see" attitude, building tension and finally showing a positive result.

State the selling points in reverse. Begin with the least important selling point. One by one add other features and benefits, but save the best for last and write that socko clincher in the very last line.

Hold the viewer's interest with accelerating pace, excitement in copy, rapid camera work and well coordinated sound effects. Check yourself with the following:

1.  Am I writing about a common problem?

2.  Am I really aware that every viewer has a problem of some kind?

3.  Have I built the commercial with expectancy? Every viewer wants to be a winner.

4.  Have I emphasized the reward of performance for every viewer who buys the product?

Emphasize the name of the product.
WRITE A "WILL IT OR WON'T IT" TELEVISION COMMERCIAL.

# WILL IT OR WON'T IT?

| VIDEO | AUDIO |
|-------|-------|
| MCU CAMERA TRACKS WOMAN WALKING AROUND KITCHEN TABLE. | Breakfast is hurry-up time during the week . . . but on the weekend my family wants a big first meal. Usually pancakes or waffles. That part's all right. But the syrup! The bottle, a cruet, a pitcher . . . always drip and drop on the tablecloth. Now there's PRIDE Syrup. |
| ECU PLATE OF PANCAKES. | |
| ECU SYRUP SMUDGES ON CLOTH. ECU BOTTLE OF PRIDE SYRUP. | |
| ECU PRIDE POURING FROM BOTTLE ONTO PANCAKES. | Look . . . Pour right from the bottle . . . |
| ECU PRIDE FLOWING INTO CRUET. ECU PRIDE POURING INTO A PITCHER FROM SOME HEIGHT. | Into a small cruet, or a large pitcher. |
| ECU LIP OF PRIDE BOTTLE. MCU CHILD POURING SYRUP ON WAFFLES. MCU WOMAN HOLDING BOTTLE PRIDE SYRUP. | No drip but easy flow. PRIDE Syrup with the new no-drip lip. Even the little ones can handle it with no drip. PRIDE Syrup— the only flavored sweetener that flows with no drip. Serve your family . . . with PRIDE. |

Some agencies want shots numbered and some do not. It is a good idea to include one commercial with numbered shots in your portfolio. This is particularly true if you have a commercial with the quick cuts we've just used in the PRIDE commercial. You will see how it should look in the following example.

# WILL IT OR WON'T IT?

| VIDEO | AUDIO |
|---|---|
| 1. MCU CAMERA TRACKS WOMAN WALKING AROUND KITCHEN TABLE. | Breakfast is a hurry-up time during the week . . . but on the weekend my family wants a big first meal. |
| 2. ECU PLATE OF PANCAKES. | Usually pancakes or waffles. That part's all right . . . But the syrup! The bottle, a cruet, a pitcher . . . |
| 3. ECU SYRUP SMUDGES ON CLOTH. | always drip and drop on the tablecloth. Now there's PRIDE Syrup. Look. |
| 4. ECU BOTTLE OF PRIDE SYRUP. | |
| 5. ECU PRIDE POURING FROM BOTTLE. | |
| 6. ECU PRIDE FLOWING INTO CRUET. | Right from the bottle . . . into a small cruet . . . |
| 7. ECU PRIDE POURING INTO A PITCHER FROM SOME HEIGHT. | or a large pitcher . . . |
| 8. ECU LIP OF PRIDE BOTTLE. | No drip but easy flow. PRIDE Syrup with the new no-drip lip. |
| 9. MCU CHILD POURING SYRUP ON WAFFLES. | Even the little ones can handle it with no drip. PRIDE Syrup |
| 10. MCU WOMAN HOLDING BOTTLE PRIDE SYRUP. | . . . the only flavored sweetener that flows with no drip. Serve your family with . . . PRIDE. |

## *Analysis*

Every homemaker is aware of the problem of sticky substances on table linen and on the shelf of a storage cabinet. Husbands and children are familiar with the sometimes too loud admonitions that follow spills, however unintentional. Here, we've found a product that has been packaged in a container that solves the problem. We are not really selling the syrup for its flavor, thickness or easy flow. We're really selling the design of the lip of the bottle, which eliminates a problem for the homemaker, and we've demonstrated that it goes into any serving piece and even works for children. We've attempted here to encourage a family get-together, a taste treat, no problem for the homemaker and a no-mess, no-criticism meal for children. Please notice that we stated the problem and hinted that maybe pancakes aren't often served because of the "syrup mess."

At the end, we've told you the "why" of the difference in our product and its competitors. We have sold a benefit in combination with enjoyment.

# ▪24▪    C'est la Vie

The vignette-of-life commercial is almost a mini-soap opera. The difference between a segment of one story line in a soap opera and a life-situation commercial is one of length. These commercials are popular because they offer an answer to a problem that many people may have. Viewer and product identity is established immediately.

You are familiar with some examples.

The ring-around-the-collar problem occurs at the wrong time, but it can be solved with this detergent. Spots on glassware are discovered just before dinner guests are expected. Such a "tragedy" could have been prevented if only a certain dishwashing powder had been used. If you're about to go out for a romantic evening, you can use this mouthwash, brush your teeth to dazzling brightness with this paste or pop a breath-sweetening mint into your mouth. You have a choice as to the best method of being kissable. None of the above is meant to be facetious. People care about these things and your commercial about a particular product may help a viewer overcome discomfiture about a problem. Keep the situation genuine. Emphasize the name of your product.
WRITE A VIGNETTE-OF-LIFE COMMERCIAL.

## C'EST LA VIE

| VIDEO | AUDIO |
|-------|-------|
| MCU TOWEL-WRAPPED GIRL SITTING ON EDGE OF BATHTUB. | Imagine! Me, with athlete's foot. I didn't pay any attention to the itching and burning at first and then came the little |
| CUT TO ECU ANTIFUNG BOTTLE. | blisters. I got ANTIFUNG right away. First, I bathed my feet and dried them thoroughly . . . |
| ECU FEET. HAND WITH APPLICATOR IS APPLYING ANTIFUNG. | then I applied ANTIFUNG all over my feet . . . including between my toes. It dried right away. The itching and burning stopped on contact and after a |
| MCU LEGS AND FEET. (GIRL WIGGLES TOES) | week of daily applications, the blisters and all the discomfort were gone. I use ANTIFUNG |
| MCU CLOTHED GIRL HOLDING BOTTLE OF ANTIFUNG. | twice a week now . . . to protect my feet. ANTIFUNG . . . to keep you walking tall and easy. |

## C'EST LA VIE

| VIDEO | AUDIO |
|-------|-------|
| MCU GIRL LEANING OVER A TABLE TALKING INTO CAMERA. | Imagine! Me with athlete's foot. Sure, I walk around the apartment barefoot sometimes, play a lot of tennis in my faithful old sneakers, shower after my exercise class and change my leotards for pantyhose after ballet class . . . and there's just no way I could get athlete's foot. Everything I have is clean. Everyplace I go is clean . . . so how could I get athlete's foot? Well, I did, and |
| CUT TO ECU ANTIFUNG BOTTLE. | so a friend told me about ANTIFUNG. I put it on and |

MCU GIRL AT TABLE
TALKING INTO CAMERA.

the itching stopped on contact.
I kept on using it and finally
those pesky blisters went away.
If I get it again, I'll sure use
ANTIFUNG. If your feet itch
and burn, you might get some.
Maybe it will help you, too.

### Analysis

We are talking about a common problem with people who engage in any sport, fail to rest their shoes between wearings or simply do not bathe every day or dry their feet carefully.

In the first commercial, our victim lets us in right where her ablutions take place. She tells us the symptoms; the name of the product; what she did before using the product; the immediate and long-range benefits and the continuing use of the product as a preventive measure. We've sold a product about an unexpected and seldom discussed problem.

In the second commercial, our friend enumerates so many ways she could have contracted the problem, we don't really care. She protests, but resentfully admits that she had the problem. Grudgingly, she talks about the immediate relief, but she makes us think she had to use it for a very long time before the condition was cured. She doesn't give us any instructions as to what to do before using the product; suggests we MIGHT get some because MAYBE it will work. The bottom line of criticism is that it took her too long to get to the product and its benefit, and she was then vague and lacking in enthusiasm. We can't sell with this one.

# ▪ 25 ▪     Simile

Simile is defined as partial resemblance. Comparison by similarity in function but dissimilarity in structure best describes this commercial. In other words . . . "as dew refreshes the rose, so DERMATEX moistens your skin."

Keep your simile simple and familiar. Having stated the simile, continue with declarative sentences about the need for the product, how to use the product and the results of usage.

You can refer to your simile at the end of the commercial if you do so briefly and remember to tie it in with the emphasis of the name of your product.

WRITE A COMMERCIAL USING A SIMILE.

## SIMILE

| VIDEO | AUDIO |
|---|---|
| MLS WOMAN AT DRESSING TABLE SMOOTHING MOISTURIZING CREAM INTO HER FACE. | No matter where you live, your skin needs a moisturizer that reaches deep down layer after layer to keep the cells fed, the tissues lubricated and your complexion soft and smooth. |
| QUICK DISSOLVE TO WOMAN WIPING A DINING TABLE WITH REVIVE. | Your furniture needs to be fed and lubricated too. I use REVIVE. REVIVE contains no wax or acrylic to accumulate and film your furniture. (VO) |
| ECU TABLETOP WITH A CLEAN STREAK AND DULL UNDUSTED PART. | REVIVE picks up dust and smudges and brings out the natural patina of wood. Do something nice for the complexion of your furniture. |
| MCU WOMAN HOLDING BOTTLE OF REVIVE. | Get REVIVE. It cares about your furniture. |

### *Analysis*

In our commercial using simile, we have related a household product to a cosmetic. Every woman is aware of the need for a skin lubricant that softens and smooths and discourages the look of premature aging. Women relate to this comparison with a household product that does a routine job ("picks up dust and smudges") and gives furniture a "beauty" treatment and nourishment at the same time.

In our sample commercial, we've given the homemaker an opportunity to buy a product that has benefits that exceed those of competitive products. We've given her help and pride in her chore and made her feel superior in the care of her home.

Keep your simile plausible. Association with a condition, place, situation, object or experience with which the viewer can identify is essential.

# · 26 ·    Dream a Little

Fantasy may be an unreal image commercial like the Pillsbury dough man, the ho-ho-ho Jolly Green Giant or the Keebler elves who make the cookies.

Coax your viewer into a moment of escapism combined with belief. Animation is often used in fantasy. *The World of Disney,* while a program, is a fine example and the memory of the Disney cartoon characters who went through all kinds of unbelievable experiences and came out unscathed can serve as a springboard for your own fantasy commercial.

Every viewer likes escapism, but in a fantasy commercial, the imaginary must be identified with reality. The reality is the product you are selling.

Your fantasy is really a fairy tale that comes true with the acceptance of the product you are selling.

If you use a symbol in combination with camera tricks, you must establish a strong relationship with the two. The gentle flying white dove was an excellent tie-in with the mildness of Dove dishwashing liquid and the white tornado is still soaring out of the bottle of cleaning fluid.

In the fantasy commercial, make the selling point with restraint, but progress to consumer satisfaction for a particular reason of product performance.

Emphasize the name of your product.

WRITE A COMMERCIAL OF FANTASY.

## DREAM A LITTLE

| VIDEO | AUDIO |
|---|---|
| MLS WOMAN STANDING WITH VACUUM CLEANER. | WOMAN<br>I've been over this carpet three times and it still looks dull and flat. |
| MLS MIDGET MAGICIAN STANDING IN FRONT OF WOMAN.<br>WOMAN REACTS WITH SURPRISE. | (SFX SOUND OF RUSHING WIND) |

| VIDEO | AUDIO |
|---|---|
| MCU MAGICIAN (SWIRLS CAPE). | **MAGICIAN**<br>I'm UPMORE, The Great. I can brighten that carpet and make the nap stand up tall. |
| | **WOMAN**<br>How? |
| MCU MAGICIAN WITH CAN OF UPMORE SPRINKLES POWDER. | **MAGICIAN**<br>With my magic UPMORE Powder. You vacuumed . . . I sprinkle. |
| MLS UNATTENDED SPONGE MOP GLIDES OVER CARPET. | **MAGICIAN VO**<br>The magic wet mop rubs it in. |
| ECU CLOCK HANDS MOVE HALF AROUND. | Wait thirty minutes, |
| MLS UNATTENDED VACUUM RUNS AROUND. | vacuum again . . . presto. |
| MLS WOMAN ON KNEES STROKING CLEAN RUG WITH FLUFFLED-UP NAP. | **WOMAN**<br>It's clean. Fluffed up. Just like new. Oh, Mr. UPMORE. |
| MCU WOMAN LOOKS AROUND. NO ONE THERE. | Mr. UPMORE? |
| ECU CAN OF UPMORE FLIES INTO WOMAN'S HAND. | Mr. UPMORE. You're a man who keeps his promise. |

## DREAM A LITTLE

| VIDEO | AUDIO |
|---|---|
| MLS BOY SCOUT CAMP. DOLLY IN TO INT. TENT FOUR BOYS ON COTS. | **1st SCOUT**<br>What's the matter, Joe? |
| | **JOE**<br>Can't sleep, chigger bites, sore shoulders from my backpack and it burns where I skinned my knee. |

2nd SCOUT
I'll get the scoutmaster.

CUT TO ENTRANCE OF TENT
AND MLS OF WITCH.

WITCH
Wait, I can fix it.

MCU OF WITCH IN CENTER
OF TENT. SCOUTS REACT
WITH FEAR.

JOE
Who are you?

WITCH
I'm the good witch. My name is
Hazel.

JOE
Hazel? Witch? Witch Hazel? Aw
c'mon.

WITCH
It's true. I live in a tree near the
Dickens House. They call me
DICKENS Witch Hazel. Watch.

DISSOLVE TO MISTY FOG
OBSCURING SCOUTS.

WITCH
There. How do you feel?

CUT TO 2 SHOT.

JOE
OK. No itch, no muscle pain and
no burn on my knee.

WIPE TO SCOUTS ON TRAIL
WITH SCOUTMASTER IN
EARLY MORNING.

SCOUTMASTER
Benson, we found a bottle of
DICKENS Witch Hazel in your
tent. Where did you get it?

CUT TO TREE. EYE WINKS
FROM BARK.

JOE
Someone must have left it, sir.

WIPE TO BOTTLE OF
DICKENS WITCH HAZEL.

ANNCR VO
For bites, stings and bruises,
sunburn and a dozen other
uses ... DICKENS Witch
Hazel.

# DREAM A LITTLE

| VIDEO | AUDIO |
|---|---|
| MCU SLEEPING GIRL AWAKENS TO SEE TOOTH FAIRY. | **GIRL**<br>Who are you? |
| MCU GLITTERING TOOTH FAIRY. | **TOOTH FAIRY**<br>I'm the tooth fairy. |
| MCU GIRL SITTING UP IN BED LOOKING AT TOOTH FAIRY. | **GIRL**<br>I'm too old for that. I'm sixteen. |
| MCU TOOTH FAIRY HOLDS OUT HAND WITH PLAK-OFF. | **TOOTH FAIRY**<br>But you still need me. I brought you some PLAK-OFF. |
| MCU GIRL STANDING WITH TOOTH FAIRY. | **GIRL**<br>But I have a toothpaste I like. Makes my teeth white and cleans my breath. |
|  | **TOOTH FAIRY**<br>But what about your teeth? All that candy, soft drinks, fun food and smoking, too. PLAK-OFF does everything your toothpaste does and more. PLAK-OFF removes all the stains and buildup of plaque that makes all those cavities your father has to pay for. Gotta go now, but try my PLAK-OFF. |
| WIPE TO GIRL BEFORE BATHROOM MIRROR. | **GIRL**<br>My teeth *feel* cleaner. They're just as white and my breath is cool and sweet. |
| MCU GIRL AT BATHROOM MIRROR. | Thanks, Tooth Fairy. PLAK-OFF is just what I need for clean, white, healthy teeth. |
| DISSOLVE TO BOX OF PLAK-OFF. |  |

### *Analysis*

We have three examples of fantasy. The first commercial has a fantasy figure who is less related to the product than the second commerical, but it is believable escapism and it does solve a problem and offer a bonus benefit.

The witch hazel commercial may be considered "corny" by some, but children will love it. The product is an old product that has many uses. If it has any faults, it is that we've mentioned three benefits from its use. It has about fifteen. There are other hair rinses, other gargles, and other sunburn remedies.

We've emphasized the benefits of this product that are not over-exposed in advertising and have fewer competitors for the benefits we've mentioned.

In the toothpaste commercial we've offered a fantasy of a product usually associated with young children, but we are relating it to an older group that needs dental care quite as much as the very young. A beloved figure returns to emphasize care as well as appearance.

We have avoided straining credulity too far.

We've taught people that one product comes from a tree.

We've solved problems and given consumer satisfaction.

We've put our products in a setting that matches their performance.

There is little else that can be accomplished.

The big DON'T of a fantasy commercial is to create a character or situation that cannot be remotely related to the product.

The big DO of a fantasy commerical is to be entertaining.

# ▪27▪    Personality

The personality commercial uses an actor or actress who plays a role. The serious authoritative character who talks about cough medicine is meant to suggest a doctor even though the commercial doesn't say so and there's no white coat in sight.

The actress who talks about a perfume or toilet soap implies that the viewer's use of that product will improve her appearance and acceptability. If the viewer infers that the purchase of the product will transform her into a ravishing, desirable beauty, that's not the fault of the manufacturer, the advertising agency, the writer or the performer. Viewers believe what they want to believe about a product and writers of television commercials don't make promises that products can't keep.

As you must "suit the action to the word," so you must match your chosen personality with the product.

Cast your own character. Write a description of the person you'd like to speak your words and convey your feelings. Ask yourself:

> What does he or she look like?
> What is he or she wearing?
> Is the product compatible with a performance of—
>> Glamour?
>> Authority?
>> Aloofness?
>> Warmth?
>> Comfort?
> How does the performer speak?
>> Confidentially?
>> With self-assurance?
>> As a teacher?
>> As a friend?

Your video must be very specific as to the shots you want and the way you want your writing performed.

Visualize! Visualize! Visualize!

Repeat the name of the product throughout the commercial, or the personality may overshadow what you are selling.

WRITE A COMMERCIAL FOR A PERSONALITY.

## PERSONALITY

| VIDEO | AUDIO |
|---|---|
| ECU CAROL WHITNEY. | Hello. I'm Carol Whitney. When you see my films, I'll bet you'd never guess I have the kind of hair poets write about but no one wants. Fine. Silky. Porous. |
| MCU CAROL WHITNEY AT DRESSING TABLE WITH BOTTLE OF CARESS. | That's why I use CARESS Hair Conditioner every night. When I'm making a film, I get a shampoo and set; sit under a hot dryer; |
| MCU CAROL WHITNEY WITH STYLIST SPRAYING HER HAIR. | and have lots of spray after the comb-out. |
| MLS CAROL WHITNEY ON SET. | Then I'm under the lights all day. |

| MCU CAROL WHITNEY COMBING HAIR. | At the end of the day my hair is dry and stiff, so I shampoo gently and comb CARESS through my hair, right to the frizzy ends. |
| ECU CAROL WHITNEY HOLDING BOTTLE OF CARESS. | CARESS is right for my kind of hair. So if you're one of those fine-haired ladies like me, use CARESS. It gives body to your hair and leaves no greasy film. CARESS . . . for you and me. |

## Analysis

Our personality, the actress Carol Whitney, talks about an aggravating problem shared by many women. When we see an actress in a film with every hair in place at all times we think she never has a problem. We assume she has a staff of hair stylists to keep her hair healthy and beautifully coiffed. We can identify with Carol Whitney whose fine hair is shampooed, set, sprayed and baked under the lights all day only because she talks about fine hair. Our commercial convinces us that if she can wash the goo from her hair every evening and comb through a product (CARESS) that doesn't leave a film and gives body to flyaway hair, we should buy it. We have solved a problem for our viewers and they have probably inferred that CARESS will make them look like Carol Whitney. The writer has defined the benefits of the product and that is the extent of his responsibility. Many performers will not lend their names or faces to products that they have not tried or seen demonstrated. Cynicism is not always in order.

## PERSONALITY

| VIDEO | AUDIO. |
|-------|--------|
| ECU TOM MILLER. | Hi. I'm Tom Miller. I won the Master's last year for the first time and no matter how long I play golf, that's got to be the thrill of a lifetime. I've learned a lot, and one of the things I've learned about is the superiority of CHAMPION golf balls. Maybe you think a golf ball is a golf ball. It's not. |

| | |
|---|---|
| ECU CHAMPION BALL. | CHAMPION golf balls are light, well balanced and durable. It's not a superstition with me. I won't play in a tournament without |
| FILM TOM MILLER ON COURSE. | CHAMPION. I can't always make them go where I want them to, but I know no chips, indentations or other imperfections are going to spoil my shot if I'm playing |
| ECU TOM MILLER. | with CHAMPION golf balls. You try 'em and maybe I'll see you on the course. |

### *Analysis*

This commercial has particular appeal to the male and female golfer. Every player is looking for a way to improve his game. Since CHAMPION golf balls are "light, well balanced and durable; without chips, indentations or other imperfections," a golfer may want to buy them. None of this is written with tongue in cheek. Many people wouldn't know about the excellent products on the market without television commercials. Unique selling points that salespeople in stores don't know or don't bother to tell us are pinpointed in television commercials. There are many exceptions, but some commercials do give information and buying guidance.

In this commercial we've given consumer service, encouragement through identity with a professional and a little bit of hope. Who knows? Maybe the next time out our golfing viewers will not hook or slice and that's fine with the manufacturer and advertiser.

## PERSONALITY

| VIDEO | AUDIO |
|---|---|
| ECU LISA JOHNSON. | Hi. I'm Lisa Johnson. You may not know my name, but you've seen my face on the cover of a lot of magazines. I guess I'm the youngest professional model. It's not easy. I make rounds, go on shootings and I |

MCU LISA JOHNSON WITH
BOTTLE OF PENBUBBLE
SHAMPOO.


MCU LISA APPLYING
SHAMPOO.

MLS LISA IN TUB WITH
LATHERED HAIR.


MCU LISA TOWELS HAIR.

ECU LISA HOLDS PENBUBBLE
BOTTLE.

have to keep up with
schoolwork. I have to wash my
hair every night and I don't
have much time. So I use
PENBUBBLE Shampoo.
PENBUBBLE is gentle, with
lots of lather, and I let *it* do
the work. That's what a
shampoo is supposed to do. I
pour on PENBUBBLE, work it
into suds and let it clean my
hair while I take a bath. You
don't have to rub a good
shampoo . . . PENBUBBLE
penetrates oil and soot for you
. . . right down to the scalp. I
rinse it off . . . towel it dry . . .
and I'm ready for bed. Get
PENBUBBLE . . . the shampoo
that does the work for you.

## Analysis

In this commercial we have a personality who actually works in
a profession to which many teen-agers aspire. The young will look,
listen and believe. Our Lisa Johnson inspires good grooming in
young viewers, identifies with the demands of schoolwork and her
profession, and offers a solution. We are giving information and
inspiration. Our shampoo "penetrates oil and soot" and it does
the work of cleansing while our busy and meticulous young women
do something else. We appeal to vanity, inform and help our
viewers save time.

Think of other ways you could write this commercial. Who is the
viewer? What are her interests? What are her activities? What else
could she be doing while our shampoo "does the work"? Grooming her fingernails? Hand-washing a favorite blouse? Talking on
the phone to the young man who's a soprano one minute and a
baritone the next because his vocal chords are thickening? Think
of your target viewer. Know her.

Write a commercial for each structure as you go through the
book. Don't copy the samples. They are meant to encourage and
guide you. Think up your own products, product names and benefits you'd like to have from such a product.

## PERSONALITY

| VIDEO | AUDIO |
|---|---|
| ECU CHARLIE TAYLOR. | Hi. I'm Charlie Taylor. I'm the catcher for the Mill City Blues. Maybe you think ballplayers smell sweaty all the time. Well, |
| MCU TAYLOR WITH JUG OF YACHT CLUB AFTERSHOWER. TAYLOR SMOOTHES SOME ON FACE. | I don't. I use YACHT CLUB Aftershower. It's a splash-on lotion you use after shaving and showering. Oh, I like flowers but I don't want to smell like one. YACHT CLUB has a clean, fresh smell like an ocean breeze at high tide. YACHT CLUB Aftershower. Use it on your face, your body ... all over. |
| MCU TAYLOR WITH YACHT CLUB. | YACHT CLUB Aftershower. It's number one with me. |

### Analysis

Charlie Taylor is a familiar sports figure with many admirers. Our "personality" does his job well and cares about that extra touch that gives him social acceptability when he isn't playing ball. The most macho viewer will feel perfectly comfortable using the same body lotion Charlie buys. We've given viewers a look at Charlie's private life and preserved his image! Imitation of and identity with an admired person have been encouraged. Sports fans and participants now know it's all right to smell like something other than rubbing alcohol and liniment. Blue-collar workers and insecure white-collar workers will probably buy our product. No man would be self-conscious about smelling like an ocean breeze at high tide.

# ▪28▪   Timing

So far, we've merely presented technique and examples of different commercial structures. There has been no consideration given to time because that is a refinement of writing, but it is the most important element in the writing of anything for television. Split-second timing is required. You will get some practice in the next chapter on Spin-offs.

As a general rule a ten-second commercial may have about 25 words. A twenty-second commercial around 45 words. A thirty-second commercial usually has about 65 words; forty-five seconds will run about 100 words and sixty seconds may be as much as 125 words. It is a good plan to mention the product name at least three times in a thirty-second commercial, but that is not a hard-and-fast rule.

# ▪ 29 ▪    Spin-offs

Spin-offs are abbreviated versions of an original commercial. You are NOT rewriting a commercial. You are editing. You can't just pick out words. You must use whole sentences and the video must relate to the audio. The video must be sequential and tell a story on its own.

If you want to try your hand with storyboards, a spin-off is a good way to do it. A ten-second spin-off or commercial will have no more than two frames; a twenty-second spin-off or commercial will have four frames at most and a thirty-second spin-off or commercial may have five frames but not more. Choose the commercial you've written very carefully so that your video does not exceed these guidelines.

Do spin-offs on THREE commercials you have written.

Sixty-second commercials are seldom written today. On-air time is too expensive, so let's concentrate on what you will actually be writing, thirty-second, twenty-second and ten-second commercials.

Notice the examples of spin-offs done on the thirty-second personality commercial with Charlie Taylor, the baseball player.

## TWENTY-SECOND SPIN-OFF

| VIDEO | AUDIO |
|---|---|
| ECU CHARLIE TAYLOR. | Hi. I'm Charlie Taylor. I'm the catcher for the Mill City Blues. I use YACHT CLUB Aftershower. |
| MLS TAYLOR WITH JUG OF YACHT CLUB AFTERSHOWER. | It's a splash-on lotion you use after shaving and showering. |

TAYLOR SMOOTHES SOME
ON FACE AS HE LOOKS IN
MIRROR.

| | |
|---|---|
| MCU TAYLOR WITH YACHT CLUB. | YACHT CLUB Aftershower has a clean, fresh smell like an ocean breeze at high tide. YACHT CLUB Aftershower. |

## TEN-SECOND SPIN-OFF

| VIDEO | AUDIO |
|---|---|
| ECU CHARLIE TAYLOR. | Hi. I'm Charlie Taylor. I use YACHT CLUB Aftershower after shaving and showering. YACHT CLUB has a clean fresh smell. |
| MCU CHARLIE WITH YACHT CLUB. | YACHT CLUB Aftershower. It's number one. |

## INCORRECT TWENTY-SECOND SPIN-OFF

| VIDEO | AUDIO |
|---|---|
| ECU CHARLIE TAYLOR. | Hi. I'm Charlie Taylor. Ballplayers sweat a lot but not me. I use YACHT CLUB Aftershower. |
| MLS CHARLIE ON BOARD CRAFT. | YACHT CLUB has a clean, fresh smell like an ocean breeze at high tide. No flowery smell for me. |
| MCU TAYLOR WITH YACHT CLUB. | YACHT CLUB Aftershower, the splash-on lotion. It's number one with me and all the guys. |

What's wrong with the above spin-off? It's not a spin-off. We changed the copy and we put Charlie out to sea for the second shot. We can't do that. We can only work with what is on the reel for the thirty-second commercial. We cannot change one word or the video even if we have better second thoughts. The key word is edit. Please notice that we've taken out whole sentences for the correct copy on the twenty- and ten-second spin-offs and we've kept the video as it was on the original. The above spin-off is technically impossible.

Straight pitch commercials are easier to handle as spin-offs, no matter how abundant and complicated the video may be. Dialogue commercials are not easy to edit into a spin-off. Writers usually know the exact assignment they have. Seldom, if ever, at this point in television, will a writer be asked to do a sixty-second commercial that will later be edited into a spin-off. The order usually carries a specific time allotment. Local markets that produce local commercials vary in their practices, however, and it's important to practice doing spin-offs. Your versatility is a strength and I urge you to include spin-offs in your job-hunting portfolio.

# ▪30▪ Interviews

The writer may be asked to do the off-camera interviews for the talking head (on-camera spokesperson). The first rule to remember is that the writer is the representative of the viewer. The interviewer must ask questions that would not occur to the layman but that interest the layman.

But that does not mean that the interviewer should not be aware of what the viewer would ask if he were there. Try to imagine the audience for your interview. If you are interviewing a political figure, there may be a member of the senior generation who will want to know whether the politician is really going to try to improve things for the elderly; whether history will repeat itself or whether this is just another person seeking a position, power or publicity. The young political science student will want to know whether or not the politician has any really innovative ideas. Is he liberal or conservative? Is he making promises the very structure of the bureaucracy will not allow him to keep? . . . and so on.

Begin the interview with general questions and work up to the big question.

Most television interviews are not scripted, but you must furnish a list of questions for the on-camera interviewer and a wealth of source material that you can only hope he will read. Avoid forming questions that can be answered with a yes or no. There is nothing more agonizing for the on-camera interviewer than a subject who answers in monosyllables.

A sports figure may be asked questions about training and technique. The politician must be persuaded to give answers and opinions he would prefer to withhold. A politician has two opinions. One is that of the people who elected him and the other is his own.

The three secrets of interviewing are conflict, hidden meaning and facial close-ups.

Go to the interview well prepared with research and quotations if possible. Pinpoint contradictions, but be certain you are familiar with the laws of libel and slander.

1.   Have a specific subject in mind.

2.   Know the life of the subject.

3.   Know something of others involved in the story.

4.   Know the history of the subject.

5.   Know the significance of the subject and have some resolution to offer.

The interviewer must have curiosity and be able to draw people out. LISTEN and comment on answers you get and be certain to ask what the viewer wants to know. Not everyone communicates well. Remember that the interviewee must be more interesting than the interviewer.

Frame your questions so that the interviewee does most of the talking. Some interviewers give their subjects very little opportunity to say anything. You, as the writer, can't control this, but you can try if you phrase your questions with words such as *explain, discuss* and *clarify*.

Certainly watch out for people who may be interesting for all the wrong reasons.

Actors may "audition" when they are interviewed and politicians may try to list their accomplishments or promises. The focus must be on what is being said, not on the personality or special interests of the interviewee. If the producer has booked a girl with a shaved head and a speech defect, you have a challenge to say the least.

All you can do as the writer is establish good rapport with the on-air interviewer. As I said, most radio and television interviews are not scripted. Some on-air interviewers will do their own research, but that is not usual. Most rely entirely on the off-camera interviewer-writer. Some guests insist upon having a list of questions presented to them before they go in front of the cameras. This happens when the guest has something in his personal life about which he does not want to be questioned. Few politicians are interviewed by talk-show hosts. Politicians are interviewed by a panel of seasoned journalists who are introduced by a host-moni-tor. The host-monitor watches the time to see that it is equitable for each journalist and that there is time for the wrap-up (closing summation) of the interview, as well as time for commercial breaks if there are any. If you are a political science or journalism major you may want to attempt this if you can find a public figure who will allow you to interview him. My students interviewed each other, favorite professors or townspeople who would consent to give them time.

As a professional, my own on-air and on-camera interviews were with writers, actors and actresses, musicians, community leaders, heads of federal agencies, people with unusual occupations and doctors who had a health message for listeners or viewers. This is the usual assignment you will have.

For reasons that you will understand later, I will give you an outline of an off-camera interview with a writer who was inter-viewed on the air by a talk-show host. I will not mention the name of the writer or interviewer. Nor give you any clues, because of the end of this experience.

I spent three hours with the writer, who was one of the stars of the golden age of television but had turned to print and published his first book. He was scheduled on the show for the purpose of promoting his book.

Here is the outline I pulled out of my files.

### NAME

Introduction to live audience.
Ad-lib greeting.
Decision to become writer.
Preparation (education and experience).

You've written a book *An Even Dozen**—what is that about? (Book is an anthology of twelve short stories.)
I first heard of you as a writer for television when the great dramas were live. You won an Emmy for *On Our Block** another for *Boot on the Ladder** and you had two series that are now in their third reruns, *Over the Edge** and *Steps in Time. * Now you've written a book. Why aren't you writing for television?
Did you have a reason for wanting to write a book?
Do you plan to write another?
If you aren't going to write a book, what do you want to do?
Why don't you write something about teen-agers, young adults and the changes we see?

---

*Fictitious names.

DO NOT ASK HIM ABOUT HIS TEEN-AGE DAUGHTERS. WILL NOT TALK ABOUT FAMILY OR PRIVATE LIFE.

You are lecturing on campuses; what is your impression of the students? Are they brighter?

This story in your book *Good-bye Child*\* . . . is that a true story?

Why did you write it?

There's another one in *An Even Dozen,*\* your new book by Baker House, about marital conflict. Where did you get the idea for that?

You seem to be interested in space travel, but this story you've called "Foresight"\* is beyond my wildest dreams. Do you really believe this will happen?

NAME will be in the book department of FOWLER'S\* Department Store starting tomorrow and all this week between twelve and four. Pick up a copy of *An Even Dozen*\* . . . wonderful reading from NAME. . . .

Thank NAME.

Break.

Would you like to know what happened? The talk-show host had a copy of the book two weeks before the writer was on; the outline was in his hands a week before the scheduled appearance and when the show aired, the questions were on the TelePrompTer.

The talk-show host did not work well with any of the writers. He knew it all. When he greeted the guest writer, the host reminded the guest of a dinner they had attended. The camera picked up the fact that the guest didn't want to remember; the talk-show host went on with a recitation of the menu, other guests, bits of conversation and a crude reminder of an accident by a waiter. THE BOOK WAS NEVER MENTIONED nor any reference made to his autographing sessions! The talk-show host completely ignored all notes and the frantic gestures of the floor manager and the producer who finally sat on the floor in front of the TelePrompTer. The book did not sell well. I can only hope this fine writer, a generous man with good camera presence and much to say, did better on other programs in other cities.

Neither the viewers nor the studio audience had the slightest idea why this man had been invited on the program. The writer said only, "That's right," "I think I remember," "Hmm mm," and several times, "about my book . . ." Guess who got the flak from the writer? There was nothing I could do and nothing you can do in a similar situation. On the other hand, I booked, researched and did the off-camera interviews for another talk-show host who spent about two hours with me while I briefed him on as many as five

\*Fictitious names.

guests, seldom referred to the TelePrompTer and remembered everything I told him. The first talk-show host is looking for a job and the second is still on.

Call or write someone for an interview.

Write an outline of the interview.

Write a list of questions to be submitted to your guest.

Script the interview.

Since I don't know your subject or your questions, I can't write it for you, but set it up like this:

INTERVIEWER

Introduction

INTERVIEWEE

Response

INTERVIEWER

Establish reason for interview. First question.

INTERVIEWEE

Answer.

etc.

INTERVIEWER

THANK YOUR GUEST AND REPEAT THE PROMOTIONAL REMINDER IF THERE IS ONE.

DON'T SIGNAL THE END OF A SCRIPTED INTERVIEW WITH THE WORDS "I see our time is up." That happens in an ad-lib interview, but it's inexcusable in a scripted interview, which some people prefer for radio. It is 1980 and scripted interviews are rare. Ad-lib interviews are usually more spontaneous, but they can sometimes be disastrous. Furnish the on-air interviewer with plenty of material well in advance of the interview. You have little to worry about if the program is taped, but there are still a few live interviews around especially in the smaller markets.

# ▪ 31 ▪   The Narrative

The writer of the narrative must be the set designer and the casting director as well as the performer. Visualization of every detail of the production and extensive research must be accomplished before the first word can be written.

The three essentials of every narrative are the character or characters about whom the story is told, the plot or action of the story and the background of the incident or incidents and the settings.

Obviously, when writing for print, there will be much descriptive writing, detailed passages that set the scene and background information that explains the psychological makeup and experiences of the characters leading up to the incident or incidents.

Much of this is expressed in radio with sound effects but we are still learning about television. In television, writers are often tempted to use description with each of these elements, but description is used only if it explains the story or advances the action.

The first item to be determined by the writer of the narrative is, Why am I writing this story? The next decision he must make concerns the result he wants to achieve. Is it fear, disgust, surprise, entertainment or little-known facts about an individual or occurrence?

Once the writer has clearly thought about those two matters, he must determine who he is. Is the writer telling the story as an observer or is he telling it from the viewpoint of one of the characters? Professionalism dictates that the narrative will be presented from the point of view that affords the greatest interest.

If the writer decides to present the narrative as an observer, then changes his mind and presents the narrative from the point of view of a character or characters, the shift of perspective must be made very clear.

Some writers clutter the narrative with details that are not germane to the narrative or with insights that he understands but that are not understood by his audience.

The safe rule is, include everything that makes your narrative complete and omit everything that is not absolutely essential. Don't become involved with mechanical actions of the character or characters. It isn't important that a character walked the full length of the room and sat down. The video shows that.

In a well-written narrative, one incident does not follow another. One incident causes another. Life itself is cause and effect; choice and consequence; whether or not any of us likes to accept that concept and that responsibility. The writer of the narrative has the greatest opportunity to make those points.

If you must include periods of time that are relatively uneventful, wrap them in a succinct paragraph or, better still, a short, declarative sentence.

Your narrative is a sequence of events. Let your viewer and

listener enjoy himself. Let him interpolate what happened between the events.

Keep your viewer constantly in mind. You cannot be all things to all people. Your narrative will interest some viewers and bore others to channel switching. That's how ratings are made.

These are some secrets that will help the writer to catch and hold the interest of the viewer.

1.   Write about incidents having to do with places, persons or conditions with which your audience is familiar or about which viewers may fantasize.

2.   Incidents concerning the home life, social scene or business of your audience will hold most if not all viewers.

3.   Appeal to the desire for escapism of your viewer by writing about romantic, unusual or bizarre incidents. Narratives about space travel, scientific projections and experiments can be challenging and usually find a ready market.

4.   Shared human-interest narratives always have a large audience. Don't shun the simple, familiar, intimate incidents to which all people can relate.

5.   Subtly introduce conversations. Depend on the video. Don't revert to the silent-movie technique of moving lips and a voice over that says, "Then she confronted him with it and she said that. . . ." "He blushed and stammered, 'It didn't mean anything. It was an impulsive act.' . . ." You are writing for television. You speak only when your characters don't.

Open your narrative with an introduction of your character or characters. Identify the location. Where did this incident or these incidents take place? When did this take place? After that you may explain why this narrative is being told through sight and sound.

Now that I've told you that, you will discover for yourself that it is not always possible or even advantageous to follow the same order of the usual narrative. You may want to relate the middle of your narrative to catch the attention of the viewer and then go back to the incidents that led up to it.

Don't leave any gaps and don't introduce any incidents until you have hinted that they are to follow and be developed.

Brisk is the word for most narratives, but that really depends on the subject and action suited to that subject.

If you are trying to express fast action follow these suggestions.

1.   Give the facts. Omit all nonessentials.

2.   Keep your sentences short and to the point.

3.   Use one- or two-syllable words.

4.   Choose diction that will convey enthusiasm and excitement so that the narrator will speak with energy and animation.

When you want your narrative to move at a leisurely pace, reverse the technique just outlined.

1.   Fill your script with details.

2.   Write long sentences.

3.   Choose words of many syllables and those that suggest slow motion. There is a different reaction to the words *jog* and *shuffle.*

4.   Establish a mood that signals the narrator to speak calmly and slowly.

Every narrative has mood. It may be humorous, nostalgic, sensational, mysterious, whimsical, intricate or intriguing.

For our purposes, we will first look at a narrative about a place. In the sample, we'll see that the film is shot to match the audio. For this reason, let's look at the copy *only,* for it is the words that count in a narrative. Notice that there is the writer's input of impressions and observations.

A documentary differs from a narrative in that one word added to fact destroys a documentary. While narration is observation; documentary is pure and simple fact. Narrative may be used in a documentary as the inner thoughts of a person, but there must be documentation of a letter written at a later date, a reliable conversation with a believable person or perhaps a diary. Not so with a narrative. Today, the live remote during a newscast is documentary if it embraces interviews with witnesses or authorities at the scene of a disaster. The narrative contains facts but is heightened by the perceptions and emotional reactions of the writer. Since you are not the cameraman nor was I on this assignment, I want you to look only at the copy before we analyze a narrative on a person.

Two and a half hours from New York and fifty cents will take you back to the turn of the century and the age of affluence that only a few can remember and some can't even imagine.

It's the Harkness estate of 235 acres outside Waterford, Connecticut, which was the summer home of Edward and Mary Harkness. It's now known as Harkness Memorial Park, but it was called Eolia. Eolia was an appropriate name for this luxurious mansion and grounds set on a breezy promontory overlooking the Sound.

The island of Eolia was the home of Eolus, the wind god, and only the Harkness estate matches the happy and luxurious kingdom that

Ulysses used as a hideaway from the strains and pressures of his homeward odyssey.

The forty-two-room Italian-style mansion was begun in 1902, and in 1950 when Mary Stillman Harkness died, the estate consisted of twenty-seven buildings, several cottages, a large greenhouse where rare and beautiful flowers are constantly nurtured, a vast garage with a turntable for the easy parking of the limousines, thirty apartment rooms for servants and a club section for bowling, billiards and squash. On the estate are stables, a large house for the manager of the estate and many smaller buildings. But with all of this, it's the grounds that hypnotize.

The marble colonnaded patio, cool and serene with the service bells at an arm's length—which once summoned a butler with a silver tray of refreshing beverages—the four English boxwoods over two hundred years old; and the Italian formal gardens that bloom from early spring to late fall, make you feel that it all belongs to you. There's a smaller garden with rare Chinese sculpture that's constantly ablaze with exotic plants in vivid colors; the fragrance of little-known herbs and the quiet reflection pools that lift their clear faces to yours.

The sixty servants who once maintained the estate have gone and now you see only the gardeners as they go about the endless job of trimming, planting and pruning. Under the trees sit men, women and children eating picnic lunches and looking down the manicured lawn that slopes into the sea. A few walk through the meadow to the beach and watch the boats sail by or toss a line for a plentiful catch that they'll clean, then cook on one of the hibachis.

All of it began as Eolia, now called Harkness Memorial Park, where time stands still; children laugh with the joy of freedom with safety and you get it all together almost instantly in this retreat that embraces yesterday and today. Harkness Memorial Park, the signs say, but it's really the home of the wind god.

The narrative is written for the sole purpose of explanation. Even if you begin in the middle, a narrative has a beginning, a middle and an end. Clarity of thought and flow characterize the skillful writer of narration.

The narrative is often used over film and it can introduce feature news as well as drama. The narrative may be historical, factual or fictional, but it is always informative and evocative of some emotion.

## NARRATIVE OUTLINE

### HERNANDO CORTEZ
Description of appearance of Cortez.
Commissioned by Cuban governor.

Malinche.
The Tiaxcalans.
March on Tenochtitlán.
Montezuma.
The retake.
Expedition to Honduras.
Life as marques del Valle de Oaxaca.
The last days of Cortez.

## HERNANDO CORTEZ

He was handsome. Of average height, his slim, lithe body moved with the speed of his piercing brown eyes, which were always dancing about. . . . always looking for something and seeing everything. Hernando Cortez or Hernán Cortés had the reputation of being the most daring of the Spanish conquistadores. Cortez first came to attention in Hispaniola for his bravery in conquest and his skill in the ring, and for his grace and footwork with the foil. Many had felt the surprise of his sharp sword and it was he who was chosen to go to Cuba. Cortez quickly won favor with the Cuban governor, Diego de Velásquez and was commissioned to conquer Mexico.

There he met Malinche, the beautiful Indian girl, whom he loved. They met, and this girl with the silken skin, brown as the earth in summer and eyes with a fire that matched his own . . .

You can romp awhile with this one, as long as you remember the time (1519) and the fact that Malinche converted to Christianity after Cortez had used her to further his own ambitions and satisfy his lust for a beautiful woman.

This is a good start for research. Remember that you must keep the outline of fact while putting in your own observations. What drove the man? What was the reason for the constant unrest? Why was he never satisfied and why did his life end as it did?

I can't take you by the hand to the library, but go and read everything you can. Take skeleton notes of facts and as you read, listen to your own responses and write those. Make an outline of the facts with subheads of your reactions and put your narrative together.

CHOOSE A PLACE, PERSON OR PERSONS OR CONDITION, AND WRITE A THREE HUNDRED-WORD NARRATIVE. Go further if you like. It's good practice, but if you keep it tight enough, the person who reviews your portfolio will read all of it. It isn't a great historical novel. It's a narrative for television.

Lacking pictures for slides, actors and actresses will "portray the parts." We've used physical description in the partial sample on

Cortez. The right casting, acting and camera work may eliminate the need for that. Concentrate on the inner emotions more than on the appearance; more on the political situation and motives than on the actual events and you will have a narrative.

Keep this in the back of your mind. You may want to use this as the basis for an episodic drama. Don't forget the growing importance of short historical dramas in television for children.

# • 32 •        News

Broadcast news unlike a newspaper has no editorial policy, or so they say. A straight newscast may be followed by an editorial that is the "opinion of the management," but the newscast itself will not editorialize. It must be remembered that there are four different types of news reporters in broadcasting. There is the "rip and run" reader who merely mouths the stories as they come off the wire services; the newscaster who will rewrite the material from the wire services, or write observations of an assignment that required an interview or trip to a site; the news commentator who broadcasts news with some personal comments of his own; and the news analyst who gives factual and balanced news reports without editorial comment.

As a writer, you don't have to think about the news "reader," but learn to distinguish between the on-air persons who "deliver" the news.

He or she is a reader, newscaster, commentator or analyst. The professional newsperson will look for significance as against simple interest; be objective; have a sense of the newsworthy; must select and order items. He must have a broad background to give setting and implications and consequences; a curiosity to probe for facts behind stories; GOOD TASTE; and the ability to maintain balance between suppression and morbid sensationalism.

It has been said that in America news is secondary to salesmanship. "There has been a grave development in Egypt and we shall give that after this message."

One of the most irritating viewer experiences is hearing a series of stories announced as "coming up right after this," waiting for a particular news story and never seeing or hearing that news that piqued his interest and kept him waiting. This is usually a problem of time and production, but it should be avoided if possible. Some magazines sell because of misleading cover titillations. Television is too ethical for that.

The purposes of a news program are journalistic. It is authoritative. Not all of the major stories of the past years were created by
television. The failure of any communistic country to feed itself
may be the fact of the century, but it may well be better suited to
magazines and books. On the other hand, a newspaper can explain
that the mainland Chinese are living on four hundred calories a
day, but television shows hunger. The aim of news takes the viewer
to the scene of the event. It does not merely record.

In writing news, the first rule is, If you don't need it, don't use
it. Ask yourself if it is important to the story and if it is interesting.
There are slow news days and busy days. The writer must adjust
his judgment to the total flow of news.

You may have a story of a quarrel between two congressmen. A
story of an explosion may break just before air time, so the writer
will want to retype the opening copy of the quarrel and cut it down
so that news of the explosion or tragedy can be given more time.
A writer will ask how much time he has and he is referring to how
long he has to do a particular story, not what time is air time. The
amount of time allotted for a story may be allocated in advance by
the producer.

News writers assume that the audience has a low threshold of
boredom that few features are able to overcome. They are right.

In news stories look for:

Significance as against interest
Objectivity.

There can be problems. The camera may not reach full speed
when the speaker begins so that the opening words are cut, or the
camera may run out of film before the statement is completed.

Always put the most important facts first, followed by lesser facts
in descending order of importance.

The first sentence always contains the five W's (who, what,
where, when, why) and sometimes "how." The headline tells the
story in miniature. The five-W lead retells it more clearly and with
detail. The next paragraphs or so provide a further retelling with
still further detail. The remainder of the story may retell it again
in chronological form with additional detail.

There is a thing called "pad" copy, which is news items added
to a script in case the timing of the writer is off, the newscaster is
off, or in case of some other emergency.

Watch out for words that look all right on paper but are not all
right on the tongue.

There are similarities between radio and television news writing, but when film is shown, the words must relate to the picture and even silence is sometimes a part of the television script. Sound will not take care of itself in television.

Remember that writing is a way to transmit information, attitudes and emotion from one brain to another.

Clear writing will produce a competent news writer but not a great one.

Strive for:

Descriptive verbs. These are usually active, not passive.
Give a narrative a beginning, middle and end when possible.
Use sentences that build until the last word.
Use metaphor and simile without clichés. Use a figure of speech only if you have a reason.
Repeat.
Be informal.
Energize the copy.
Personalize. (The city council raised OUR taxes.)

Watch for rhyme and meter. They belong to poetry—not news. A trick you can use is to count each syllable above one per word in a sentence. Take a second look at any sentence that has a score above twenty.

For instance:

a one-syllable word is not counted
a two-syllable word counts one
a three-syllable word counts two
a four-syllable word counts three, and so on.

Make two sentences out of one. Take out adjectives and any superfluous words.

The daily news show begins at the assignment desk. Assignment editors work from newspaper and wire service stories, police radios, telephoned tips and their own instincts for news. They assign reporters and camera crews to cover the events of the day. Film of these events is then rushed back to the station for processing. Then the writer enters the picture. The program producer assigns him to one or more film stories to handle. He screens them with a film editor and they work together choosing the pictures and sound to be used and the order in which they are to be spliced together. The editor does the actual cutting of the film, but the writer supervises. If the reporter in the field has supplied a complete narration, all the writer does is write a lead-in for the story, such as: "Centerville's public schools opened again for the fall term—Reporter John Smith has that story."

As in commercials, only the right-hand half of the page is used for air copy. Each half line of forty characters is figured at two seconds.

Pictures tell the story. You will have a spot sheet which the film editor prepared, or you may have to do it yourself.

| LS | building on fire | :04 | :04 |
|----|------------------|-----|-----|
| MCU | flames | :02 | :06 |
| CU | flames in one window | :04 | :10 |
| MS | fireman with hose | :06 | :16 |

Do you understand that? We've begun to cover a fire and since we've allotted only sixteen seconds for this part of the video, obviously we are going on to the removal of victims, interviews with those who escaped and friends of those who didn't. We've given four seconds to a long shot of the building on fire; a medium close-up of the flames two seconds (now look at the second column —it's cumulative—so we've now used six seconds). We zoom in for a close-up of the flames in one window for four seconds. The total time is now ten seconds and we cut to a medium shot of a fireman with a hose. We'll stay on him for six seconds, making a total of sixteen seconds. This is a spot sheet.

Do not be confused. The following chart is not one for a news program. It is for a typical prime-time (between 7 and 10 P.M.) format of a network program. Start with a certain time—perhaps 9 P.M. Add the length of time as outlined and make a second column of cumulative time. Once you put this on paper you will be more at ease. Watch television without being absorbed in the program. Time each segment of the show until you are familiar with how crucial it is to write within a framework of time.

| Length | Segment |
|--------|---------|
| :30 ⎫ Pre- | Network promo |
| 1:30 ⎭ program | Local promo/commercial/commercial |
| 3:30 | *Program time*/teaser/main credits |
| :10 | Opening billboard |
| 1:00 | Commercials 1 & 2 (30/30) |
| 11:20 | Program segment |
| 1:00 | Commercials 3 & 4 (30/30) |
| 12:38 | Program segment |
| 1:00 | Commercials 5 & 6 (30/30) |
| :42 | Local break promo/commercial/ID |

| 10:00 | Program segment |
| 1:00 | Commercials 7 & 8 (30/30) |
| 12:00 | Program segment |
| 1:00 | Commercials 9 & 10 (30/30) |
| 1:00 | Trailer |
| 1:00 | Commercials 11 & 12 (30/30) |
| :40 | Credits (voice over promo) |
| :30 | Public service promo |
| :30 | Network promo |
| 1:02 | Local promo/commercial/commercial/ID |
| — | Local news program |

You cannot write a thirty-five-second script to a piece of film that runs only twenty-eight seconds or the last seven seconds will be read over black.

One network insists on five years' experience on a major newspaper or wire service, but they will now hire people with five years in local television only, if that person is really good.

Another network looks for people with college degrees (a must nearly everyplace) and preferably a degree in journalism. They want a minimum of two years' experience in an active television station news operation. This must include experience in writing to film, supervision of film editing as well as nonfilm news writing. Experience on a college television station doesn't count.

A third network insists that you take a writer's test. It is tough. At this network, stress is on print experience, and a person who has worked exclusively in electronic journalism will not be hired. Here, you must have three to seven years of good solid reporting on a large daily newspaper or wire service in a major metropolitan market. If the candidate has electronic experience on top of that, so much the better. This network will hire people with two or three years of college if the experience meets their requirements.

Networks want wide news experience. If you are asked if you've been out on the street with a camera, you can be reasonably certain you aren't going to get the job. Explain that you are a writer, not a cameraman. It probably won't help. You are being put down. Talk about what you have done and mention that you are on the interview to offer your talent and experience as a contribution to a team effort, not to list those skills that belong to others. Sometimes it works.

Be certain that your samples are not written in literary style.

Stick to simple declaratives with minimal use of adjectives.

Don't use compound and complex sentences.

WRITE A THIRTY-MINUTE NEWSCAST CONTAINING: international

news, national news, local news, a feature (food, consumer, medical, fashion, celebrity), sports, weather and human interest.

Since much of a newscast is composed of live on-the-scene reports and taped and filmed stories prepared in advance, the writer
often has little to do except write headlines for on-air news reporters. A few on-air newscasters write their own material so your
writing will be confined to whatever the assignment editor gives
you to do. You have the instructions concerning HOW to write, so
I'll give you some typical examples of the composition of a network
(national) newscast and a local thirty-minute news report.

In the first schedule there was one in-studio newscaster who did
very little except introduce filmed accounts to supplement a few
sentences about what the viewer was about to see.

Following you will see an outline of the stories presented in a
national newscast.

## OUTLINE OF THIRTY-MINUTE NATIONAL NEWSCAST

   I. Revolution in a foreign country. Total time   4:30
      A. Filmed report of actual take-over.
      B. Reporter from our nation's capital with official reaction.
      C. News analyst with background information leading to the
          revolution.
  II. Report on worldwide athletic event and our national participa-
      tion. Time   2:00
 III. Commercial break
      (Usually two thirty-second commercials or three twenty-second
      commercials.)
  IV. Report on political caucus of Party A.
      (Three reports from three leading contenders.) Time   4:00
   V. Commercial break
  VI. Report on political caucus of Party B.
      (Two reports from two contenders.) Time   3:30
 VII. Commercial break
VIII. Report on appointment of prosecutor to investigate national gov-
      ernmental corruption. Review of charges. Time   2:30
  IX. Commercial break
   X. Report on a small town protesting the building of a nuclear plant.
      Planned march on nation's capital. Time   3:30

### *Analysis*

In this simplified outline of content only, the news is international or national and related to our national interest.

Occasionally, there will be a human-interest story at the end of the newscast, but this is true only if it's a "slow" (not much happening of significance) news day.

National newscasts usually follow a local newscast and if the local news team is weak or incompetent, you may be sure the ratings of the national newscast on that station will be low.

Since your assignment is for a thirty-minute newscast including news that is international, national, local, feature (food, consumer, medical, fashion, celebrity, sports, weather, human interest), let's assume you write for an independent (one without network affiliation) station. It's a lot more fun because you can include anything and everything.

Suppose you're writing a newscast on the same day as the national newscast just outlined. There's a revolution in a foreign country and it might lead to our involvement. BUT, in your city, a fire is raging out of control in a factory that employs thousands of people in your area. Also, the city controller shot and wounded his wife. Rumors have circulated about this and a few bulletins have been telecast.

What are you going to do? Are you going to tell me about the revolution in a foreign country and make me wait to hear about the fire in the factory where my husband and family work, and following that the story of the wounded woman? The fire and shooting are local events and you serve your community by putting community matters first. If the United Nations building in New York collapses, that's something else. Not every skilled newscaster and news writer works in New York. Pretend you live in one of the great cities outside New York, Los Angeles or Chicago. First, tell me about the fire. The income of many of your viewers is affected. How are you going to tell me about it? Will you begin your story with: "Thousand of workers will be jobless because of the fire in the Merson Chemical Company that has been burning for five hours"? NO.

"Fire continues to rage at the Merson Chemical Company after five hours. John Wilson is there now and we switch you there for a live report."

Probably, you won't get to write more than that.

Wrap up the story with information about the company and perhaps a statement from an executive of the company about plans for the future. Don't forget to promise your viewers you will keep them informed of new developments.

Now, I want to hear about the woman who was shot. Are you going to write: "Mrs. Pearson Dean is recovering in Mercy Hospital from a gunshot wound inflicted by her husband"? Who's Mrs.

Pearson Dean? I haven't much interest in politics or city officials and I'm a viewer who gets most of her news from television, so you'll write: "Police arrested Pearson Dean, city controller, after he shot his wife during a quarrel at their home on Brentwood Avenue. Dean was taken into custody this morning. . . ."

Now I know who, what, where and when. Tell me why. What were they quarreling about? How long have they been married? What have the neighbors observed about their relationship? Are there any children? Where are the children? What is the physical condition of the victim? Where is Dean? In jail or out on bail?

Unless the person involved in the story is very well known, it's usually a good idea to write "what" first. If the "who" is an official but not a celebrity, please tell me what position he holds. What is his title?

Don't give me a "soft" involved lead. Hit me with words like *fire* and *police* and I'll stay tuned.

Let's take a look at an itemization of stories taken directly off the air of one local thirty-minute newscast.

## OUTLINE OF LOCAL NEWS

I.    Fire in local chemical plant.
II.   City official shoots wife.
III.  Revolution in foreign country.
IV.   President proposes increased defense spending.
V.    House approves change in federal tax laws.
VI.   Governor orders investigation of purchasing fraud in maximum-security prison.
VII.  Private plane lands safely in local park.
VIII. City school teachers strike and mayor comments.
IX.   Drug raid in adjoining state. Possible sales in this state.
X.    Local hospital needs volunteers for weekend duty.
XI.   Muriel Tanner autographs new novel in local store.
XII.  State senator attacks mayor on budget.
XIII. Movie-Theater-Book-Restaurant review.
XIV.  Sports.
XV.   Weather.
XVI.  Human interest. (Keep it brief.)

In Centerville, Arkansas, an eighty-five-year-old man bit his wife again and again. She got tired of it and when the police wouldn't do anything, she stopped it herself. She threw away his false teeth.

### Analysis

In our local newscast, we've covered our city, commented on the foreign revolution (given thorough coverage on national news), advised that our president wants to increase defense spending, alerted our viewers concerning federal tax changes, reported on our governor, warned our community of possible drug traffic, served a hospital in need, promoted a book written by a popular author, revealed the thinking of a state senator, heard about entertainment to enjoy or avoid, learned the scores of sporting events, found out whether or not to take an umbrella to work tomorrow and shared laughter.

Some of the stories are merely two or three sentences long, but we've served our community and no one is going to challenge the license of the station with that kind of coverage.

In the outline of the local newscast, "special" reporters are absent. For instance, there is no consumer reporter or health and science editor. There isn't room for this every single day in a thirty-minute newscast, but either live, taped or filmed, most stations have reports on a controversial subject, a constitutional amendment yet to be ratified, a debate on gun-control laws, or a commentary on an international problem that they can insert if they need it for time.

You have an opportunity to create a niche for yourself. At one time, I was the senior writer on a talk show that featured a three-minute spot of news headlines. The reporter on the show wasn't very good and was about to be fired. I was assigned to review a play and this reporter jumped in with an impassioned speech about how many hours I worked and how difficult it must be for one person to write a daily ninety-minute show. He "offered" (begged) to go in my place to review the play. Overnight, he became the station's drama critic. He's still there and still not very good. This man makes a lot of money passing off his personal opinions as professional evaluation. I'm not suggesting you do that. I am suggesting you consider becoming a specialist in some area. Food, law, consumer goods, movies, the arts, health care or even meteorology. These pluses are door openers and provide increased security in a very insecure business. Remember, you have to be good at what you do no matter where you do it. People in small markets move onto larger cities and finally to production centers. It happens.

# ▪ 33 ▪       The PI

PI means per inquiry. You've seen these commercials. They have to do with record albums, houseplants or kitchen gadgets that do

everything but cut off the heads of your friends. The most familiar
PI's are those that advertise an album of songs by a favorite singer
or an album that features a collection of well-known songs by
different singers.

The video in a PI is very important. Usually there is a film of the
covers of the albums with a sound track of sample lyrics from each
of the selections. Done more simply and inexpensively, a roll of
titles accompanied by snatches of the melody of the songs may be
used.

The copy consists of the titles of the songs, the name of the artist
or artists; an assurance that the album cannot be purchased in any
store and a hard sell persuasive message to send so much money
for records or an increased amount for tapes to a certain address.
A toll-free 800 number is given for impulse buying. COD charges
are added to telephoned orders.

PI's are handled through direct-mail marketing companies that
buy time on various stations for the placement of the commercials
for these items.

The copy for a PI is not very challenging for the writer, but most
marketing companies employ a writer-artist-producer who creates
the entire commercial and sees it through every step of its production.

The ethical writer will try to determine the condition of the
product. Are the records scratched? Are the selections boot-
legged? Is the plant dead when shipped? Does the chopper really
dice the vegetables or is it better suited to melted butter? A good
relationship with the head of the marketing company will enable
the writer-artist-producer to know these things, and protect his
integrity. However, my personal experience has taught me not to
ask questions. Unemployment lines are not fun. The beginning
writer should avoid direct-mail marketing firms and only the experienced writer-artist-producer should attempt the responsibility
that the PI imposes upon him.

Do not make a storyboard, but write a thirty-second PI for a
record album or a kitchen gadget. Don't ridicule your product.
Some viewers of the PI's will pick up the phone immediately and
order. Remember to state that there are no returns.

PI's usually produce a surprising revenue for the marketing
company. The PI is designed for the impulse buyer: the fan of a
particular artist, the collector who is missing something from his
collection and the sentimentalist who hears a few bars from a song
that held some particular significance for him at one time. On the
positive side, PI's do provide the consumer with enjoyment of
something that is no longer available in any store. But let the buyer

beware. The percentage of complaints is often high, especially on houseplants.

Let's look at a typical sample of a PI.

## THE PI

| VIDEO | AUDIO |
|---|---|
| | ANNCR VO |
| ECU RITA CARROLL ALBUMS. | Now for the first time, the hit songs of Rita Carroll live again in two albums of your favorite songs. Not available in any store so get paper and pencil |
| HOLD TITLES. | right now. |
| | MUSIC: "WHITE ROSES" IN AND UNDER |
| | ANNCR VO |
| | "White Roses" |
| | MUSIC: SEGUE TO "IN MY ARMS"—UNDER |
| | ANNCR VO |
| | "In My Arms" |
| | MUSIC: SEGUE TO "AFTER TONIGHT"—UNDER |
| | ANNCR VO |
| | "After Tonight" |
| | MUSIC: SEGUE TO "FOR THE LAST TIME"—UNDER |
| | ANNCR VO |
| | "For the Last Time" |
| | MUSIC: SEGUE TO "FOOLISH ME"—UNDER |
| | ANNCR VO |
| | "Foolish Me." Yes all of these, |
| SLIDE #3 RITA CARROLL. | plus nineteen more of the songs of the incomparable Rita Carroll including |
| | MUSIC: "FOOLISH ME"—OUT |
| | ANNCR VO |
| | "Try Me," "Vacant Room, Empty |

SLIDE #1
800-123-4567
SLIDE #2
RECORDS $6.95
TAPES $8.95
RITA
BOX 111
GRAND CENTRAL STATION
NEW YORK, N.Y. 10017
JASON MARKETING
COMPANY
AMES, IOWA

SLIDE # 1
800-123-4567

Heart," "Miracle Time," and others. All the songs you know and love. Keep Rita Carroll a living legend . . . but hurry. Supplies are limited. Never again will you hear the warm voice of Rita Carroll except in your own home. Not available in any store, anywhere. Order now. Call toll-free 800-123-4567. That's 800-123-4567. Pick up the phone now or send six ninety-five for records, eight ninety-five for eight-track tapes to Rita, Box 111, Grand Central Station, New York, New York 10017. That's Rita, Box 111, Grand Central Station, New York, New York 10017. Add three dollars for postage and handling. But call toll-free 800-123-4567 right now for Rita Carroll and save the postage and handling.

The name of the marketing company will be at the very bottom of the film or slide, but it's there. If you are one who buys records this way, always watch for it. You'll soon learn which company is careless about quality; the length of time it takes for delivery and whether or not you'll have to write several letters after you get your canceled check before you get your merchandise. If you can possibly live without these issues and are unfamiliar with various marketing companies, go to your local record store, and substitute something else. Some marketing companies are very ethical indeed; some make very human mistakes and some write very interesting letters to complainants. I've been lucky in the purchase of PI offers. I've also worked in a direct-mail marketing company.

### Analysis

In this PI we appeal to the emotions of the viewer. A deceased singer's hit songs are available as a special issue.

Reread the copy before the sample. You will find all of the elements of a PI that produce sales.

1. The album is not sold in stores and is available only by phone or mail order. Lucky and special viewer.

2. The operators are waiting for the viewer's call. Treat the viewer to impulse buying.

3. The album is by Rita Carroll, the viewer's all-time favorite singer. The viewer is a fan.

4. The album contains the selection "Miracle Time" and that's the only Rita Carroll recording some viewers don't have. They are collectors.

5. The album has a recording of "Vacant Room, Empty Heart." Some viewers have just split from a lover. An apartment seems like a tomb and the viewer feels like a dry well. The viewer or viewers in that experience will buy the album to hear Rita Carroll express their feelings.

If our PI had been about a houseplant, we would probably have endowed it with magical powers of good luck. If we had written a PI for a vegetable peeler, we direct our copy to the homemaker who just cut her finger with a paring knife and has a husband who complains about thick peelings and the loss of nutritive values in the carrots.

PI offerings are very satisfying to some viewers, and persons who work in direct-mail marketing companies work very hard indeed.

# ▪ 34 ▪ The ID

The ID is the identifying phrase for a station. It isn't used much anymore, but if you are lucky and get a job in a small station, you may be asked to write one. Every station used to have one. Some examples are:

WXYZ—your community-minded station.
WXYZ—at the crossroads of America.
WXYZ—at the gateway to the West.

Most independent television stations have an ID on a slide above their logo. One New York independent has the words YOUR CHOICE above the channel number.

One of my comedians at the university wrote an ID that announced, "This is station KASS, at the end of your dial."

The other students loved it and laughed long and loudly while I had to put on my station manager's hat, frown and lecture him on the importance of image, dignity, good taste and a projection of the philosophy of the station.

Your station's ID is extremely important to management and to the community. You can write an ID that is dynamic and memorable, but don't try to be funny or ridicule your station.

WRITE AN ID for an imaginary or local station.

# ▪ 35 ▪   The Institutional Commercial

Every corporation operates within the climate of public opinion. Institutional advertising reflects the philosophy, integrity and quality standards of a company as expressed in scientific achievement, management activities or manufactured products. You are selling a name that means certain things.

Institutional advertising informs but does not persuade. It is always dignified, reserved and restrained. The purpose of the institutional commercial is to enhance the reputation of the company and build goodwill toward that company. The writer does not promote specific products or urge the viewer to go to a dealer or store.

WRITE A THIRTY-SECOND INSTITUTIONAL COMMERCIAL.

## INSTITUTIONAL COMMERCIAL

| VIDEO | AUDIO |
|---|---|
| MCU STORE EXECUTIVE OR ACTOR OF DIGNITY IN STORE SETTING. | There are no salespeople at WINSTON'S, only interior designers. WINSTON'S designs your home to suit your needs and taste. Every piece of furniture at WINSTON'S is individually selected for quality from the creations of the most skilled craftsmen. Whether you want to design one room or your entire home, you can be assured of quality. Visit the home of WINSTON, so we can help you with yours. |

## INCORRECT INSTITUTIONAL COMMERCIAL

| VIDEO | AUDIO |
|---|---|
| MCU STORE EXECUTIVE OR ACTOR OF DIGNITY IN STORE SETTING. | There are no salespeople at WINSTON'S, only interior designers. WINSTON'S designs your home to suit your taste and budget. Whether you want to design one room or your entire home, it doesn't mean you'll pay more. In fact, at WINSTON'S you'll probably pay less. Come to |
| DISSOLVE TO SLIDE EXT. ENTRANCE OF WINSTON'S. | WINSTON'S. You'll be surprised at the quality and prices. |

### *Analysis*

In the first commercial, we have announced the availability of service and quality in a very understated way. We've let you know that WINSTON'S is a store of quiet good taste. We've "sold" the store to those who demand the best and to those who aspire to the best.

In the second commercial, what have we done? Naughty. Naughty. We've mentioned "budget," "pay less" and "prices." We've had the *chutzpa* to say "come." We destroyed our image of superiority by talking about money and persuading people to come. Commercial two is not a "pure" institutional commercial.

# ▪36▪     The PSA

The PSA is the public-service announcement. It may be commercial or noncommercial. The public-service announcement is related to institutional advertising. It is designed to move ideas instead of products and is supportive of human needs and aspirations. The writer of the public-service announcement must have an attitude of understanding and altruism in behalf of the welfare of people.

A public-service announcement may be about forest fire prevention or the use of seat belts. The PSA may urge you to send money to CARE, the USO, the Heart Association, the Arthritis Foundation or the college of your choice.

Most advertising agencies contribute billions of dollars in creative time, talent and production facilities through the nonprofit organization known as the Advertising Council, which places these announcements. Networks and stations are very cooperative in bringing these messages to the public and there are no more useful reminders.

WRITE A TWENTY-SECOND PUBLIC-SERVICE ANNOUNCEMENT.

## PUBLIC-SERVICE ANNOUNCEMENT

| VIDEO | AUDIO |
|---|---|
| ECU LINDA COOPER. | Hello, I'm Linda Cooper.* Every year, multiple sclerosis cripples thousands of Americans and confines them to a future in wheelchairs. Please send your contribution to your local Multiple Sclerosis Foundation to help find the cause of and cure for this tragic disease. |

## PUBLIC-SERVICE ANNOUNCEMENT

| VIDEO | AUDIO |
|---|---|
| ECU JOHN SMITH. | Hello, I'm John Smith, executive director of the Boy Scouts of America. The many programs in scouting enable thousands of boys to learn skills, how to get along with other people and participate in sports. Call your local Boy Scout headquarters and find out how you can participate. Thank you. |

*We are to assume that Linda Cooper is a well-known film actress. Celebrities usually do these public-service announcements for scale (the lowest amount their particular performing union allows). Most of the time the "star" contributes the money to the charity for which he or she performs or to the Theatre Authority, the clearinghouse for the stars who appear in behalf of a cause.

There's really nothing wrong with this announcement except people are more likely to respond to a celebrity or a freckle-faced boy than to an executive like our nice mythical "John Smith."

Watch these announcements. Some begin with "*This* is John Smith," "Linda Cooper." I can't think of any person as a "*this.*" While it may be used in radio on the premise that a voice is not distinctive enough to be recognized, a face on the screen is something else. Write: "Hello, I'm NAME."

Have you been noticing that the right margins of our audio are often uneven? Why? NEVER HYPHENATE ANY WORD OR DIRECTION ON A COMMERCIAL OR SCRIPT. It confuses the performer as well as the director. Never mind looking pretty on a page. If you don't do the final typing of your work, tell your secretary over and over again.

# • 37 • The Co-op Commercial

The co-op commercial is a commercial that mentions both the manufacturer and the retailer. The copy of the commercial is determined largely by whether the manufacturer or the retailer is paying all of the cost, 75 percent of the cost or if the cost is shared by the two. You've often seen these commercials. An example of the co-op commercial is that of a towel or bed linen manufacturer with the name of the store where it may be purchased at the very end. In this commercial, you will write about the manufacturer's product exclusively. What is the product? What makes it different? Why is it superior? Why is it a better buy? If the name of the store is mentioned only at the end, you can be certain the manufacturer is paying for all or at least 75 percent of the commercial.

A second kind of co-op commercial may be written with emphasis on the store with the name of the manufacturer of one product mixed in with the name of one or more manufacturers of other products. In this copy, you will stress the convenience of shopping at one store for everything and it may be the retailer who is paying most of the cost, or the cost may be allocated among the manufacturers.

A third co-op commercial may seem to give equal emphasis to the manufacturer and the retailer. The creative director or perhaps the salesman of the station will give you the creative direction. You will be told how many times to mention the name of the manufacturer and the retailer and be given information about the product and/or the store.

WRITE THREE KINDS OF CO-OP COMMERCIALS.

## CO-OP COMMERCIAL

| VIDEO | AUDIO |
|---|---|
| | MUSIC: IN AND UNDER |
| | ANNCR VO |
| ECU MOVING PEN WRITES THE TITLE "SIGNATURE" BY ADELE. | Adele, the world's most creative perfumer, introduces SIGNATURE . . . a perfume that is vibrant but gentle; innocent but sophisticated. |
| CUT TO ECU BOTTLE OF SIGNATURE. | As changeable as your mood. Sign yourself with SIGNATURE by Adele. It's uniquely you. MUSIC: OUT |
| | ANNCR VO |
| SUPER FOWLER'S GELLER's AND OTHER FINE STORES. | Available at FOWLER'S, GELLER'S and other fine stores. |

"Adele" paid for this one but "Adele" has to have outlets for her perfume, so they are mentioned. FOWLER'S and GELLER'S may have contributed a small percentage of the cost but it isn't likely.

### Analysis

We are emphasizing the perfumer and the product and we've written the copy to link the two. The name of the perfumer sells the scent and we've used adjectives that run the gamut of aromatic choices. The writer should test the perfume and no matter what it smells like to him, listen to the creator and use the words she uses. Where to buy the perfume is not as important as the introduction of a new fragrance by an established "name." The appeal is to status.

## CO-OP COMMERCIAL

| VIDEO | AUDIO |
|---|---|
| ECU PERFUME BOTTLE WITH QUILL PEN ON TABLE. | MUSIC: IN AND UNDER |

WOMAN VO

At Fowler's we have your
SIGNATURE. SIGNATURE by
Adele . . . a perfume that is
you. Vibrant but gentle;

QUICK CUTS OF WOMAN IN
OFFICE; PLAYING TENNIS;
innocent but sophisticated. As
changeable as your mood. Sign
DANCING AT DISCO. CUT TO
yourself with SIGNATURE. It's
ECU PERFUME BOTTLE WITH
uniquely you. SIGNATURE . . .
QUILL PEN ON TABLE.
MUSIC: OUT

WOMAN VO

. . . only at Fowler's.

The store, Fowler's, paid for this one. The manufacturer or creator is mentioned only once. The store is telling you what the product is and that you can't buy it anywhere but in *their* store. Perhaps you can, but Fowler's wants you to come to *their* store to buy the perfume and while there, the customer has to have a whole wardrobe to go with it, doesn't she?

### Analysis

In this co-op commercial, we are coming as close as we can to a "hard" sell of a perfume. We can't let the viewer forget the name of the fragrance. We repeat the name SIGNATURE for the viewers who want a new scent and hope it will give them a different image and perhaps new experiences. Subtly, we are telling viewers that this perfume will accentuate the individuality of the wearer.

Very likely, "Fowler's" is doing a thorough promotion of this perfume. Counter cards; pretty girls walking near the store entrance distributing small vials of the new perfume and scented statement enclosures complete with printed order forms. All of this promotion is supportive of the commercial.

### CO-OP COMMERCIAL

| VIDEO | AUDIO |
|---|---|

ECU HAND HOLDING
PERFUME BOTTLE.

MUSIC: IN AND UNDER

ANNCR VO

Adele introduces her newest
fragrance . . . SIGNATURE . . .
a perfume that is you.

SIGNATURE . . . only at
Fowler's. Vibrant but gentle;
innocent but sophisticated.
Adele salutes your uniqueness
with SIGNATURE . . . available
at Fowler's.

MUSIC: OUT

This is a commercial in which the cost is shared. You can count
the number of times the perfumer is mentioned and the number
of times the store is mentioned. The product name is paramount.

Retail advertising is important. Once, while I was performing
just such a commercial, the retailer telephoned me to say that he
thought I said the name of the manufacturer louder than I did the
name of his store. The advertisers are listening and looking.

### *Analysis*

This co-op commercial has the emphasis on the name of the
product supported by the prestige of the perfumer. We have added
a touch of exclusivity by mentioning that only one store has it.

In a shared cost co-op commercial, you have to count. How
many mentions of the name of the product are used? How many
times does the manufacturer want to hear his name? How often
must the name of the store where it can be purchased be written?
You'll probably be told. If not, keep the emphasis on the names
of the product and the store and wait for further direction.

Finally, here is a co-op commercial one sees with increasing
frequency. Three manufacturers have probably contributed small
amounts to the store (Cole's), but most of the cost is borne by the
retailer.

| VIDEO | AUDIO |
|---|---|
| QUICK CUTS OF MENTIONED MERCHANDISE. | ANNCR VO<br>Save energy. Yours. Shop at COLE'S, the family store. All-wool Thompson blankets; towels and bath accessories by Reltex; COLE'S own refrigerators, washing machines and dryers; Weaver shorts and shirts for men; the latest fashions for women and snuggly hooded coats for |

children. COLE'S has
something for everyone. Make
your shopping day a one-stop
day. Come to COLE'S, the
value store for everyone and
everything.

### *Analysis*

The real selling point of our "Cole's" commercial is the convenience of shopping under one roof for a variety of items for a number of people. This is one-stop shopping for every member of the family. Convenience, diversity and value are your key guidelines.

Remember, the item is the star. Keep your video on the merchandise. Indicate a VO (voice over) for the copy and hope it will go through. I really believe that an on-camera spokesperson is a distraction in this kind of commercial. Many retailers agree with me. Others think they have to have a pretty girl or handsome man. Thankfully, only a few owners and/or managers think they must be the performer. Sometimes, a salesman can't sell unless he promises to let the nonprofessional voice* the commercial and jump in front of the camera. We've all seen the results.

# ▪38▪    Overture

Every television program begins with a presentation. If you are very well known and successful, you may make your presentation over the telephone or luncheon table. If you are well known, successful and established, you won't be reading this book.

Remember that everyone has an idea for a television program. Remember, too, that there really aren't any new ideas. There are, according to some experts, only twenty-six basic ideas for television programs. I'm not even sure there are that many. What you see each season is a new way of presenting an old idea or situation.

Most producers receive about eight thousand presentations each year. There are 365 days in the year and always only ten top programs.

---

*Voice* is used here as a verb. Professionally, a commercial, "voice over" of a narrative or commercial are "voiced." The director never says "announce" to the performer. The direction "announce" is given only to "announcers" who identify a station with the call letters, tell us to "stand by" because "we are experiencing technical difficulties" or give a promo of a program that they hope you will watch.

Since we must assume that you are a beginner, the best entry is a job, any kind of job, working for a producer or a production company. Forget that you're a writer. Type, answer the phone, send out for sandwiches and coffee or just hang around if they'll let you. You'll see piles of folders containing ideas for programs, but more importantly you'll get a firsthand look at how decisions are made.

If you just can't wait and you must make a presentation of your idea, the following brief outline will give you the minimal basics of how to write a presentation.

First, write an outline of your idea in detail. This is not a part of your presentation. It is for you. It will clarify your thinking so that you can write the concise presentation that producers are accustomed to receiving.

On *separate* pages write the following.

Page 1   Write your name and address.
Page 2   Write the name or title of the show and the length. Is it a thirty-minute, sixty-minute or ninety-minute show?
Page 3   This is the "Who are you" page.
        Are you a company? If you are, write the name of the company and list other programs that you have produced.
        Are you an individual? If so, simply write your name and give a list of your professional credits—the titles of the shows on which you worked—your own title and a list of your duties.
Page 4   List the characters or participants in your show. Describe them physically, psychologically, vocationally, or if they are well-known persons, give their qualifications, titles or documented field of expertise.
Page 5   Tell your story. BRIEFLY. What is the program about? If it has a purpose, state it. If it doesn't, don't try to convince a tired overworked producer that your idea is the one the world is waiting for.
Page 6   Assuming that your program idea is to be presented once a week for thirteen weeks, list thirteen VERY short paragraphs about each of the thirteen programs.

Producers and the members of their staff are not stupid. They know instantly when an idea will "play." By following the above outline (and ideas about outlines vary), you will find greater receptivity.

Your next step is to learn the name of the producer. Telephone or write for an appointment and be willing to talk with anyone who will see you. Your brother may know the chairman of the board, but he doesn't make program decisions, and even if he makes an appointment with a producer for you, your idea is less likely to be reviewed objectively than if you made the contact yourself. Contacts are fine but don't depend on them. It's your creativity and nothing else that will get your idea on the air. Once you get that appointment, talk your presentation first, then leave a copy. Don't walk in and hand the producer a folder. The interview will probably not be long. If the producer is really interested, he will call you to come in again. Follow up, but give him time. Remember, he is doing his day-to-day job, looking at new properties, dodging political assassination and trying to find time to go to the bathroom.

No one is trying to steal your idea. The best way to prevent that from happening is for you not to talk about it. Write your presentation, make your appointment, keep your appointment and·wait.

Try to do what all producers must do. Think of others. Don't write a presentation of what you'd like to see on the air. Write a presentation for a program many people will enjoy.

Write a presentation for a thirty-minute, once-a-week show.

The following will serve as a graphic example of what your presentation should look like. You may be surprised at the amount of "white" space and the few words, but I assure you that it is quite enough to give the decision-maker the information he needs. He doesn't want to read a tome.

Page 1

---

SALLY JONES
219 East Cardinal Street
Brooklyn, New York 12345

Page 2

THE TIMES OF YOUR LIFE
A Daily Half-hour Show

Page 3

CRYSTAL PRODUCTIONS

Created and wrote:
Life of Nijinsky
View from the Fire Escape—Producer
Transformation—Producer-Writer

If you have no such credits and you probably don't, simply write
your name and any college or community theater credits you may
have. Be sure to say what you did on these productions. If this is

your first presentation, say nothing except a *few* words about why you think this is a good program idea.

Page 4

---

Sandra Holt

A 24-year-old model, mother and housewife who is the founder and owner of FITNESS HEALTH AND BEAUTY SALONS. Sandra successfully runs a business, has a second career, is a mother of two children and the wife of an attorney.

Evelyn Manning

A 46-year-old widow who is a nutritionist-consultant for a number of day-care centers, nursing homes, beauty farms and corporations.

Ann Bailey

A 68-year-old handicraft specialist who arranges exhibitions of work of older craftsmen and has a syndicated radio program on entertainment and leisure activities for the people of the third generation.

---

Page 5

---

The aim of THE TIMES OF YOUR LIFE is to enrich life for viewers of all ages. With occasional name experts as guests, we expect to stimulate a zest for life and the creative spirit of everyone. By doing this, we want our viewers to have the joy of self-discovery; to realize that it is never too soon or too late and to develop their individual potentials to the fullest.

---

Page 6

---

1.   An introductory program of skin care for all ages; a look at the feeding of infants; an introduction to painting.

2.   Makeup for the teen-ager; menu planning of day-care centers; encouraging parent inquiry and involvement and a review of a television series.
3.   Simple exercises before you get out of bed; the daily nutrients needed by all persons and a demonstration of making stuffed animals out of men's socks.

Etc.

---

That should give you an idea of exactly what you need. Save your wordage for your conversation with the person to whom you make the presentation. Be sure to have paragraphs of proposed program content for at least thirteen airings. Although this show I have presented was conceived as a daily offering, it finally aired as a once-a-week show.

The names of the on-air spokespersons have been changed. The content of your program will vary according to the time slot it is assigned. It doesn't have to be all male or all female. Some women have to function as plumbers, gardeners and electricians. There are all kinds of possibilities. You may decide to make a presentation of a game or quiz show.

# ▪ 39 ▪     Promotion

The writer may find himself in the promotion department where he will write releases on personalities and programs for on the air or the printed press. In on-air promotional spots, a short announcement urges the viewer to tune in at a certain time for a certain program with this or that star and perhaps a brief provocative description of the program content. It may or may not be accompanied by a film clip from the program. The copy may be read by a staff announcer while the video consists of a slide. Always write "tune in."

Begin the release with, "Tonight see Star Starr in 'Suns and Moons,' the story about . . ." Or, if the performer is likely to attract the audience, you will begin the spot with the name of the performer, followed by the title of the program, a brief description of the story, the time and the number of the channel or the call letters of the station or the name of the network.

The personality press release always begins with the name of the star; the few inner "facts" about the star's life or a statement concerning the contract he has just signed; the name of the program; the day, time and identification of the station or network.

The program press release will emphasize program content rather than the personalities. It will be longer than the others and "hyped." If the program is an adaptation of a novel or concerns a historical event, you have a lot of material with which to work. If it's a "sit-com" (situation comedy), you'll have to pull out the adjectives. You do not tell the entire story, but there may be a titillating sentence about a particular episode. Little will be mentioned about the performers. This kind of press release is often used when a new program series is about to be aired. Newspapers and magazines are flooded with these releases before the beginning of a new season, at a rating "Sweep" time* or when a new program replaces a canceled one. Affiliated stations receive these and are expected to promote them at the local level. Radio stations are often used to promote a program to be aired on television.

WRITE AN ON-AIR RELEASE.

WRITE A PERSONALITY PRESS RELEASE.

WRITE A PROGRAM PRESS RELEASE.

## ON-AIR RELEASE/PROMO

| VIDEO | AUDIO |
|---|---|
| FILM CLIP OR STATION OR NETWORK LOGO. | Tonight, John wants to keep a gun in the house, since David was attacked, but Valerie |

---

*The month-long audience surveys of local markets by research companies to determine how well local stations around the country compete with one another.

objects. *TONIGHT* at nine on
DIVIDING LINE. Here on ABS
—Channel 3.

These on-air releases are meant to pique curiosity and build audiences. If the viewer went bowling last week and missed the attack on David, he'll certainly tune in to find out what happens next in this modern episodic (thirty or sixty minutes) drama.

Many of these announcements appear throughout the day. Some mention programs for the next day or two days or a very special event or program a week away. Be prepared to turn out a lot of these if you are in the program or promotion department. Agencies do not prepare these announcements, only staff station or network personnel.

Review the announcement again. We've emphasized the time, named the program, reminded the viewer of the network and channel and given a hint of the program content.

## PERSONALITY PRESS RELEASE

*SERENA*
Appearing on AROUND THE TOWN—ABS—4 P.M. Monday through Friday.

Serena, America's most famous belly dancer is trimming the waistlines and limbering the hips and knees of women of all ages.

Born in Greece, the shy, gentle lady known as Serena deplores the concept of belly dancing as a suggestive vulgar display intended to excite men.

Serena, like many dancers of this art form, was three years old when she began to learn this ancient dance.

Belly dancing was intended to assist women in natural childbirth and is a series of exercises in muscular control, coordination and flexibility. It takes years to perfect the art and is an aesthetic form of athletics.

Serena has a chain of studios and frequently appears in exhibitions of her art on television and in ethnic clubs whose members truly understand and appreciate belly dancing.

Her proudest achievement is a book giving the history and step-by-step instructions of belly dancing.

Serena is married to a lawyer whose name she never mentions and has a nineteen-year-old son.

I haven't changed the name of the above personality. I interviewed her, learned a lot about her art and had the privilege of meeting a lady.

## PROGRAM PRESS RELEASE

FOR IMMEDIATE RELEASE

ABS announced today that a new series HIGH VIEW will premiere Sunday night at 9 P.M. EST—8 P.M. CST starting January 14.

The series, a sit-com about window washers in the Big Apple is rated by critics who previewed it as the coming all-time hit.

Tom Canfield and Bruce Whitman star as the two window washers who know who is in whose bedroom; what is hidden where and what to do about the naked old lady who beckons for one or both of them to come in. She's not serving tea.

Join Tom Canfield and Bruce Whitman in hijinks on HIGH VIEW for an all-time high of laughter on ABS starting Sunday, January 14.

# ▪40▪     The Big Idea

How do you get ideas for commercials, scripts and presentations? Every writer is equipped with imagination and sensitivity, but a writer must be willing to research constantly. The writer must be alert, observant and an unabashed eavesdropper. The taxi driver, the waitress in a diner during a slow period, neighbors, friends, acquaintances, strangers and most of all children, to whom all things are new. People are your main source. Listen. A word here, an observation there, can be written down and used later.

Above all, you must read. Daily papers, including out-of-town papers, magazines for all ages, special magazines aimed at specific interests, trade magazines, product labels and, above all, books. Don't confine your reading to your own interests or even your own age group. Get out and around. See movies, go to the theater, and while you may throw your back out, drop in at a disco and always stay in touch with the young. Each generation looks at the changing world in a different way, and if you don't know how they are perceiving things, you can't write for them. The elderly, or what I prefer to call "the third generation," have their story. Spend time with them. They've lived through many cycles and their memories and experiences in contrast with the young may give you just the spark you need.

Another source of ideas is our own memory. What happened to you? Where? When? What was your reaction at the time? What is it now?

Most of all, a writer must have time to dream. Oh, for the day when creative directors will realize that writers need to take a break for a walk, sit in the park, go to a movie or take a trip to a neighborhood where the socioeconomic standards are different from his own. Writers cannot be chained to desks from nine to five and be expected to be creative. Some management people and creative directors know this and give their writers freedom, but they are few.

If you can, travel. Unless you have a compatible companion, travel alone. If you can go to a foreign country, do so. Everything will be new and different to you. Explore, make notes, soak up the ambience, watch the mannerisms and habits. Even if your budget allows for domestic travel only, choose an environment totally different from the one in which you live. Talk to the townspeople and listen, listen, listen. Depending upon the location, even people in urban centers think and react differently. A New Yorker does not think or act like people in Chicago, San Francisco, Kansas City, Dallas or Los Angeles. It may seem so unless you dig for the inner perspective. If you live in an urban center, choose a small town in a different section of the country. Try to imagine that you've lived there all of your life and have never traveled more than two hundred miles from that town. Don't be condescending. Be one of them for a long enough time to absorb the pace; the prevailing mental attitudes; the hopes, dreams and fears of the people; what motivates them; and what they reject. Keep that notebook with you night and day. Listen to dialects and expressions you may not have heard before. Every person is unique. Socioeconomic status, past and present, your education, your experiences, your choices, your dreams, your triumphs, your defeats and your reactions to all of these make up who you are. There is no one like you just as there is no one like anyone you will ever meet. There is a tapestry of human threads, but each has its own coloration and your sensitivity to this gives your writing that touch that has wide appeal.

Let the creative juices flow. Strained humor, contrived situations and oblique phrases do not belong in television writing. Observe and see. Get your emotions out of the way. Be concerned with the reactions of others. Listen and hear. Accept the different and watch for it. Read, comprehend and think about how you might have written it. Watch television not as a viewer enjoying himself but as a writer who could have written it better. Make notes. Be conscious of the different reactions a character might have had. A commercial with a pretty girl is not enough. Turn your chair away from the set and listen to the words. If you liked looking at the girl, be patient. If you wait eight minutes, they'll probably run the same one again.

Keep a notebook by your bed. If you can't sleep, dream, remember, imagine. Don't struggle. If you have a dream and awaken, write it down. Your mind is a storehouse, but some things are behind locked doors or thrown out the window. Keep that notebook with you at all times and above all keep a diary without fail. That's not old-fashioned. Even if the day seemed uneventful, write at least a paragraph. If you had an uneventful day, you weren't watching or listening to your greatest source—people. Be sensitive to your own experiences. Who said what and pleased you? Who did what and hurt you? Why are you hurt? What was the motive of the person who hurt you? While that is important, it is more important to record the experiences of others. Watch the young person with his first job. How does he react to his first triumph; his first disillusionment? Watch the retiree. How does he react? What is his underlying feeling? Feel with them. Observe the hostile. Probe the enigmatic. Excavate beyond the bones and hair. Listen to the words but hear the heart. You will grow as a writer and a person.

It is never enough to know something intellectually. If you don't know it in your gut, you don't know it. The key word for all writers is identification. You cannot write with enthusiasm and understanding unless you identify with your product or your character. A can of soup may be only part of a lunch to a child or business executive. It may be a meal to the poor or elderly. A character may be pleasant because he is passively aggressive, selfish and manipulative or genuinely in harmony with people. Another character may be unpleasant because of self-hatred, inability to transcend negative experiences or to gain attention. You'll know if you look, take notes, get your own reactions and conditioning out of the way and then write it for us.

# ▪ 41 ▪    Serial and Episodic Writing

Serial and episodic writing are two different things, but since the technique for the two is the same, a distinction can be made only in the sense of time.

An *episode* is usually a story about a group of persons that is complete within itself for a certain time period. In television, episodic writing is called a "series." A certain program is aired at a certain time each week and within that thirty- or sixty-minute period, you see the same characters enacting a particular incident that has a beginning, middle and an end. A beginning in television is very brief. You set the scene and get into the situation to be resolved as quickly as you can.

A *serial* is commonly called a "soap opera." There are several story lines or plots going on within a certain time period. This couple may be having a certain problem, while another couple will be coping with a different situation. The two are interrelated from time to time as the truly skilled writer gives us a look into the personal lives of a group of people. Most "soaps" have more than one writer under the watchful eye of a head writer who supervises the development of the different story lines. A few actors have made the transition from performing to writing serials, but it is a field for only the most experienced and talented writer. It is virtually impossible to break into it. Head writers are familiar with the work of other writers or they may choose an actor with long performing experience in serials to join the writing staff.

In episodic writing, you are really writing a mini-teleplay. In serial writing you are writing several mini-teleplays simultaneously.

A course in television performance is useful to a writer as is a course in production, but the best teacher you will ever have is neither of those, nor dozens of books. The best teacher is your own television set. Don't get lost in the program. Put your attention on the camera work. If you must, you can buy books that reprint successful teleplays, but this will tempt you to copy shots that may not be the best accompaniment for your dialogue. Begin your episode with an idea. Put it on paper and you will see whether or not you have an episode or have daydreamed something that "would be nice to see on television." Write the entire story in detail. The script must describe everything your viewer will see or hear.

Where is it happening?
When is it happening?
Where should it be happening?
How should it be happening?

Is something happening in one place that is unknown to other characters in another place? If so, you must share this with your viewers.

Who is involved?

The next thing you will want to do is to become acquainted with your characters. Write vignettes of each of your characters. Constantly ask yourself questions about their psychological makeup. What has happened in their lives to mold and condition them into their outward behavior? What emotional volcanoes are bubbling inside? You will clearly define age, appearance and general characteristics, but you won't have a play if you don't know the inner person and his background and previous experiences.

You are placing these persons in a particular situation at a particular time for a particular reason.

In serial and episodic writing, you are writing for everyone involved in the presentation to the viewer. You are writing for the director, cameraman, performer(s), set designer, lighting technician, sound technician and the sound-effects man. The old rule about writing what you know about is not necessarily true in episodic or serial writing. Very likely, your characters are composites of people you've met. You literally create people. If you create a character like your Aunt Dora, endow Aunt Dora with additional mannerisms and hidden psychological characteristics that you do not immediately expose. Since no one really knows anyone else, you can't limit yourself by having your characters act and react in predictable ways throughout the episode. If you do, you destroy suspense and excitement.

In the theater, each act of a play usually has one set. A thirty-minute television episode may have four or five or even more. A sixty-minute presentation of a daily serial may have ten or more.

Like the television commercial, the episode must have an ending that resolves a problem or conflict. Your crisis comes when the conflict reaches the "fork in the road." Will your characters react as expected, or will you write a role-reversal based on a change of consciousness, the eruption of long-concealed emotions or the revelation of hidden motives or characteristics?

Before you begin to put your story into script form, clearly define to yourself where you are going. Ask yourself these questions or similar questions applicable to your story. In addition to the where is it happening? when is it happening? how is it happening? and who is involved? have a clear visualization of:

How did this situation develop?
What is the relationship of all of your characters?

In other words:

Why are these two people attracted to each other?
Why do these people remain married?
Why do these opposites remain together?

One of your characters will have the sympathy and admiration of your viewers most of the time. There must always be an antagonist or you don't have dialogue. The sympathy and admiration may shift back and forth, but your viewers will only stay glued to the television set if you glue your characters together for a reason.

If you have a "bad" guy, you should reveal what makes him that way and remember that no "bad" guy is totally "bad" and no "good" guy is totally good. Pace is important. If one of your characters has been submissive for so long that she has become emotionally immobilized, the other characters must be in constant changes of mood and action to compensate for it. Your situation and your resolution may see the protagonist win or the antagonist get his comeuppance. Happy endings used to be the only way to resolve a situation, but television viewers are now accustomed to seeing unhappy situations remain that way, while the persons involved go their separate ways and work out their own futures. This is not to suggest that you must become a tragedian to write a believable episode, but it does mean that your resolution must be logical and plausible.

Once you have your story clearly in mind or have written it in short-story form, make a list of the sequential actions that move your episode along. Each can be merely one sentence, but it will serve you in the development of your story.

Next, list the sequences of the video. You must visualize each setting, each situation and the character involved in each or you will have only a fuzzy outline of what you want to happen.

You are now equipped with your written story, the detailed vignettes of your characters, the list of sequential actions and the scenes of your episode as they evolve one into another.

You must now know how to put it all down in professional form.

Keep in mind the where, when, how and who and you will move on more easily than you expect.

Number each page in the upper-right corner with your name followed by the title of the script. You don't have to number the first page of the script, but it must state the name of your episode and your name.

First, there should be a one-inch margin around the right side, top and bottom. This serves as the frame of your script.

You will probably not be asked or expected to write a shooting script, but whether or not you are, remember that each shot is individually numbered on the left throughout the entire script.

Type the shot number about 1-½ inches from the left-hand side of the page. This is about the fifteenth or sixteenth pica space. The shot description and detailed action are written here. Write the descriptions of the shot (this is the where, when, how and who) on the same line in capital letters.

1.                              INT.   COMMON ROOM OF
                                SENIOR CITIZENS HOME:—
                                DAY—FULL SHOT—GROUP OF
                                ELDERLY PEOPLE.

Notice that the location is always preceded by INT. (for interior) or EXT. (for exterior). This tells your director how much shooting is indoors and how much is out. Observe the dashes between the descriptive elements.

Follow that shot with a *reason* for a new shot. Don't repeat all of the information in the first shot. The next shot may read:

2.                              A GROUP OF ELDERLY PEOPLE
                                SIT AT A TABLE WORKING ON
                                HANDICRAFTS.

Your script must include details of the action and this comes directly beneath the description and separated by a double space. Use single spacing for the detailed action itself and do not use capital letters for the detailed action.

3.                              ONE ELDERLY WOMAN
                                STRUGGLES WITH MODELING
                                CLAY.

                                Occupational therapist moves
                                toward woman as other group
                                members watch.

Separate the dialogue from the detailed action by a double space. Type the name of the character in capital letters at the center of the line. Write the actual dialogue under the name. The dialogue is single-spaced and is separated from the name by a single space.

                         AGNES HOGAN

                    Mrs. Collins, you must try to
                    complete your projects. We are all
                    here to work together.

                         ALICE COLLINS
                         (Apologetically)

                    I'm sorry. I've never been good

> with my hands and now my
> arthritis . . .

> ### AGNES HOGAN
> (Impatiently and loudly)

> That's just an excuse that you've
> probably used all of your life and
> you're not the only one here with
> arthritis.

If there is detailed action described between dialoque, separate it from the dialogue by a double space, but use single space within itself.

> One man leaves the table, two
> women stare at Mrs. Hogan, while
> the other three concentrate on
> their work.

If a shot is continued, write it like this:

> CONTINUED:
> The two women stare at each
> other and back at Mrs. Hogan.

You have established an ambience, a situation and the reactions of your characters.

Half-hour scripts may run from thirty to fifty pages depending on the dialogue and the action. Your characters will not be talking all of the time.

While it may seem that we have proceeded backward, it is now time to write the very first part of your script.

There must be a title page. Write the title of your script, your name, full address and your telephone number.

On the next page list the characters with a *brief* description; a list of the exterior shots in one column on one side of the page and a list of the interior shots in one column on the other side of the page. Be sure to head the list, EXT. and INT. The next page is the title of the episode and your name and after that is the first page of your script.

Write a thirty-minute episodic script.

1.   Turn back and list all of the elements outlined.

2.   Use the beginning of the episode in the senior citizens center as a trial script. How will you resolve the situation? What will you do about Agnes Hogan? Your episode must be complete

within itself. You are not writing a serial. You are writing "a moment in time" that has a resolution. You can accomplish this only if you have:

    a.   Written the entire story in detail.
    b.   Written vignettes of each character.
    c.   Written a list of the sequential actions.
    d.   Written a list of the video sequences.

As I said, a serial has many story lines going at once. Different writers are assigned to "follow" different characters through their particular situations of the moment.

I was never "spoon-fed" as a writer and I don't wish to do that to you, but I will give you four excerpts from which you can work. Remember, these are segments within different serials. They are not complete episodes.

The first situation concerns two young unmarried people who have a child and live together in a very loose arrangement. Figure out the relationships; visualize and write the video and extend it into an episode if you can. We open on a crisis.

Richard Peterson
Margaret Peterson
Larry Peterson
Michael Findley
Claire Findley
Jenny Findley
Timmy Findley

Scene:    The small apartment of Larry Peterson and Jenny Findley. Richard, Margaret and Larry Peterson are standing and walking around the apartment. Michael and Claire Findley are sitting with obvious agitation because their unmarried daughter, Jenny, is the focus of concern. Larry Peterson is holding the baby, Timmy Findley, who is screaming.

### MARGARET

Where could she be? Where could she have gone?

### MICHAEL

Who knows? Who knows anything after this last year?

### LARRY

She never did anything like this before.

### CLAIRE

Well what happened? Did you have a fight?

### LARRY

No. I just came home. Timmy was yelling. He was wet and she was gone. Just like that.

(The door opens and Jenny Findley comes in.)

### MICHAEL

Where the hell have you been?

### JENNY

Riding my bicycle. What's wrong with that?

### MARGARET

What's wrong with it? You went out and left the baby alone, that's what's wrong with it. Larry came home, the baby was alone and crying and you were nowhere to be found.

### JENNY

So, Larry called the clan to come in for a "shame on Jenny," session.

### CLAIRE

Jenny, this is serious. There could have been a fire. Timmy could have hurt himself. You can't leave him alone like that. You could have called me, called anyone if you had to go out. Why did you go out?

### JENNY

I had to get out. I had to get away from the diapers, the bottles, the burping, the silence. Nobody to talk to. Nothing. Just baby, baby, baby. I had to get on my bike and ride and ride and ride and be free. I'm just too young to be a mother.

### MICHAEL

You weren't too young for sex. What did you think would happen? A trip on a trampoline?

### LARRY

You didn't have to have the baby.

### RICHARD

That's right. We offered to pay for the abortion.

### JENNY

Oh sure. But you didn't offer to have it. Besides I wanted that baby.

### MARGARET

A baby means responsibility.

### CLAIRE

And half of that responsibility is Larry's. But oh no. Let one thing happen and he panics and calls Mommy and Daddy.

#### MICHAEL

Shut up, Claire. This won't get us anyplace. We have to figure out something. But how does a baby grow up while his parents are growing up?

Don't skip through these assignments. Write your character vignettes and keep your video moving. There's nothing more annoying than two people talking "at" each other. In this next excerpt you have to use a lot of close-ups for facial expressions, and keep Katherine moving.

In this excerpt we are about to see an eruption of a long existent situation. Katherine and David are only two of many characters in this "soap." Your challenge here is *keeping the video moving!*

Katherine Alexander
Dr. David Alexander

Scene: Interior—living room of Alexander home. Katherine is pacing the floor. She hears a key in the lock and Dr. David Alexander comes in.

#### KATHERINE

Another late night. Another late dinner. What was it this time? Phyllis Townsend suddenly couldn't breathe in her new pink nightie or you had to play musical chairs in the chart room?

#### DAVID

Please, Katherine. I lost a patient. Bill Travers.

#### KATHERINE

Oh. Sorry. Well, you knew he was dying.

#### DAVID

That doesn't help.

#### KATHERINE

It isn't your first loss and it won't be your last. Here, have a drink. I'm already three up on you.

#### DAVID

I've been meaning to talk to you about that.

#### KATHERINE

About what?

#### DAVID

Your drinking. It used to be every night and now it's every morning, too.

### KATHERINE

I didn't know you noticed.

### DAVID

Oh, I notice. I notice a lot of things. Your irritation with me all of the time. Your lack of interest in the children just when they need you most and we do have three teen-age children.

### KATHERINE

I was pregnant and delivered three times. They're not my children, and they don't have a father. You never spend any time with them.

### DAVID

I'm a doctor. I don't have any time. But they are our children.

### KATHERINE

No. I had three children for the woman you love and to please my father. My dear father who bought me a husband.

### DAVID

What are you talking about?

### KATHERINE

I need another drink. (*Pours drink*) I'm talking about the fact that the only woman you ever loved is your mother. You've spent your whole life looking for your mother. You even tried to find her in Lisa. Oh, you didn't know that I know about Lisa. Blond, buxom Lisa, the private duty nurse who gave you money during the last two years of med school. And then came Dr. Lawrence Farnsworth the second. Dear Dr. Farnsworth with a twenty-seven-year-old daughter no one seemed to want to marry. And there was handsome, brilliant Dr. David Alexander, the perfect match for daughter Katherine and the perfect protégé for .dear Daddy Farnsworth.

### DAVID

You think I married you just to move ahead? You think I didn't care about you?

### KATHERINE

I know you, David. You're chief of cardiology. Maybe you would have been that anyway. But not so soon. There were others better qualified and you know it. As for me. You didn't want me as a woman. You wanted me as the mother of your children. You never talk about me. You recite a list of all the schools I attended. The clubs I belong to and the charities for which I work, but you never say one word about me. But why should you? Katherine Farnsworth Alexander. She died but I don't remember when.

Read through this next excerpt. It is the end of what one character hoped would be a new beginning. If you like, you can write a beginning and middle for this and use this NEAR the end of an episode that has a definite conclusion.

### JOHN

Marilyn?

### MARILYN

Hello, John.

### JOHN

I wasn't quite sure.

### MARILYN

You mean an unexpected meeting with an old wife is confusing.

### JOHN

No, I didn't mean that. You just look different and seem different.

### MARILYN

Time has a way of doing both.

### JOHN

You're bitter.

### MARILYN

Wrong. I'm older and wiser and it doesn't hurt anymore.

### JOHN

I'm glad.

### MARILYN

No you're not. You'd love it if you thought I still loved you and our divorce had ruined my life.

### JOHN

You think I'm cruel.

### MARILYN

In a way. You still want to punish me.

### JOHN

You keep saying that. Why after fifteen years do you still say the same thing? WHY?

### MARILYN

Because it's true, that's why.

JOHN

How can you think that? We've been divorced for eight years and I married again and . . .

MARILYN

And divorced again.

JOHN

Oh, you found out.

MARILYN

Yes, I found out. It wasn't a very long wait.

JOHN

You sound like you knew it would happen.

MARILYN

I did.

JOHN

You and your positive predictions. But I thought we were talking about me wanting to punish you. I'd just like to get that straight . . . just once.

MARILYN

There's nothing to get straight. You shoved me out of your life and it was either get a divorce or lose my mind.

JOHN

I loved you very much. I never met anyone like you.

MARILN

But you never really let yourself go with either of those things.

JOHN

What things?

MARILYN

For loving each other intimately and completely the first night we met.

JOHN

It was wonderful.

MARILYN

It was to me. We said everything to each other, but you thought it was wrong. You think you must spend a certain number of hours with someone and have certain facts about someone before you can be in love.

### JOHN

Well, yes, of course, we have to . . .

### MARILYN

What century do you live in, John? For one moment you were
interested in what I thought and believed and what I was. For one
moment, all of the faith and love within you held you up and we
knew each other. Really knew each other.

### JOHN

I remember.

### MARILYN

But oh no. All the way you drove me home you were upset because
you didn't know my mother's maiden name and whether or not my
father belonged to the country club.

### JOHN

That's silly.

### MARILYN

No, it isn't. You were interested in a lot of facts, figures and status
surrounding me and because you didn't know them before I let you
make love, you thought I should be punished. For you, John, it's
always been too soon to say I love you.

### JOHN

Well you have to know family background and history. You can't just
go around giving yourself to just anybody.

### MARILYN

Was I just anybody?

### JOHN

No.

### MARILYN

But right away you began to push me aside. Oh you married me. You
didn't have to. I wasn't pregnant.

### JOHN

I married you because I wanted to.

### MARILYN

And right away you put me in the back room of your life along with
all of your guilts, your disappointments, your prejudices and your
condemnations and you only came around when there was no place
else to go. Right away, you put me in your past and began to look
around for a future . . . without me.

JOHN

It wasn't like that.

MARILYN

It was and it is. You did the same thing with Carol and you'll do it with the next one and the next one.

JOHN

Carol wasn't like you.

MARILYN

Of course not. She was nice. She gave you her genealogy and astrological charts and then you proposed.

JOHN

Well . . . anyway. You're the nice one. You're warm and gentle. You pour yourself out and hold nothing back just to get something.

MARILYN

That's right. I poured myself out for you. I'm empty but I'm free. I'm not looking, but you are. You're still holding out for that perfect person, that perfect situation, that perfect time to say I love you.

JOHN

I'm saying that now. You are that person. This is the time and I love you.

MARILYN
(*Very gently*)

John. It's too late.

Let me start you on an episodic drama in a series. The following will show you exactly how to begin.

Page 1

WAYFARER INN

"ONE LEG DOWN"

Mary Jones
615 East North Street
Bellmore, New York 12345

(516) 123-4567

PRODUCTION NUMBER
DATE
NAME

WAYFARER INN (Series Title)

"ONE LEG DOWN" (Title of Episode)

## CAST

DOROTHY SLATER—Waitress
SUSAN TALBERT—Waitress
CONNIE FORBES—Hostess
MACK FORBES—Owner of Wayfarer Inn
PHIL ROGERS—Banker of nearby Broadfield
DR. BURKE—County medical officer
DUKE TRACY—Truck driver
BILL GANNON—Truck driver
JOE GILBERT—Bachelor merchant of Broadfield
SHERIFF ALLAN—County sheriff

## SETS

*EXT:*

HIGHWAY OUT OF BROADFIELD
PARKING LOT OF WAYFARER INN
FRONT OF WAYFARER INN
EXTERIOR OF JOE GILBERT'S PHARMACY

*On reverse side of page*

*INT:*

WAYFARER INN
MEDICAL OFFICER'S LABORATORY
LIVING ROOM OF CONNIE FORBES
OFFICE OF BANKER ROGERS
JOE GILBERT'S PHARMACY
LIVING AND BED-ROOMS OF DOROTHY AND SUSAN, WHO
    SHARE AN APARTMENT

"ONE LEG DOWN"                                                    1.

1.  EXT. FLAT HIGHWAY OUTSIDE BROADFIELD—NIGHT
    Few stock cuts of countryside and city limits sign.

2.  EXT. PARKING LOT OF TRUCK STOP RESTAURANT—
    NIGHT   Two women come out the side entrance of the
                WAYFARER INN. We MOVE WITH THEM as they
                walk toward car.

> DOROTHY
>
> Slow night tonight.
>
> SUSAN
>
> Yeah. Not much fun except for Duke and Bill.
>
> DOROTHY
>
> Yeah. My feet are killing me. I'm glad I'm not on the swing shift this week.

3.  WOMEN APPROACH CAR. DOROTHY UNLOCKS DOOR.

> DOROTHY
>
> Oh, I forgot to take my fresh uniforms in. I'll get 'em—they're in the trunk. I'll just be a sec.
>
> SUSAN
>
> OK.

4.  WE MOVE TO REAR OF CAR WITH DOROTHY. A SHOE IS STICKING OUT.

> DOROTHY
> (*Yelling*)
> Sue! Sue!

5.  SUE COMES RUNNING. LIGHTS OF PARKING LOT SHINE ON TRUNK. POV (Point-of-view) SHOT SHOWS MAN'S SHOE STICKING OUT OF TRUNK.

> SUSAN
>
> Oh, my God, it's a shoe.
>
> DOROTHY
>
> Is there a foot in it?

6.  SUE REACHES HAND TOWARD SHOE AND PRESSES.

> SUSAN
> (*Voice trembling*)
> Yeah . . . and it's not moving.

Write the story. Pick up the video from there and list it in sequence. Follow all of the steps as outlined and you will have a full hour episode in a series.

# ▪42▪   Music, Music, Music

The air is full of it. Radio and television commercials are often selling messages set to music that fits the product. Dramas have musical "bridges" and the sound track of old movies is full of mood music that enhances the action.

But where do you come in? Are you a copywriter, producer, director and musician? Great! You probably aren't, so how do you begin as a writer in this exciting but complex part of the television business? Most jingles are written by an outside contractor who can score, write and conduct. Most agency people simply do not have all the necessary talents for this highly specialized and lucrative field.

As a writer, however, you may be asked to write lyrics that include the major selling features of the product. That's as far as you can go unless you are a composer. If you are not, once you've written the lyrics, you and the composer huddle with the producer to talk about the mood, the instrumentation, the performers and the cost as well as when the commercial is going on the air; the number of markets in which it is to be used and whether or not it is to be done on film or tape.

Once the conference is over, you, the writer, are out of it. There may be so many changes made by so many people you may scarcely recognize your lyrics or even your concept. That is beyond your control.

All of this is an oversimplification of what takes place, but just for fun, choose a product, write some lyrics and if you have a musician friend, ask him to score them for you and put it on a cassette. If you can't do all of that, just write some lyrics about a product, leave a space in the middle for a voice over by an announcer (write the announcement) and put it in your job-hunting portfolio.

I can't teach you what I don't know. I've written jingles but none was accepted. Don't be surprised if you have the same experience.

You may have a special talent for this, so try.

Write a jingle for a real or imaginary product. Indicate the type of music you imagine should accompany it. A perfume will have an entirely different kind of music from that which would be played for frankfurters or chewing gum. Mood is the key word. The mood of the music must match the product. If you take your job-hunting portfolio to a creative director and he seems interested in the lyrics of your sample jingle, whistle or hum the tune. Don't sing unless

you can, but you might describe the instrumentation or the kind
of singer you have in mind. Go ahead. Try your hand at the lyrics
for a jingle, but be sure the tune is original or at least in the public
domain.

There is no point in giving you an example of one of my jingles
that didn't make it. I didn't have anyone to score for me and using
a familiar tune that the producer didn't like seemed to be the basis
of the rejection.

I can, however, give you the guidelines and characteristics of a
jingle. You may have just the special talent for this, but be sure to
follow the basics.

## GUIDELINES TO CREATING A JINGLE

Refer to the chapter on concepts and headlines.

A jingle must first have a concept and one line that states the
most important selling point.

Answer these questions and make notes before you begin.

1.  To whom is the jingle directed?

    Men only?
    Homemakers?
    Teen-agers?
    Career women?
    Children?

2.  What is the benefit?

    Savings? Money, time or both?
    Pleasure?
    Quality?
    Taste?
    Other? Define.

3.  Does the music come first and the film cut to the music
    track? *or* Is your visual so strong you want the film first and
    the music postscored? Detail the video.

4.  What music "mood" fits the target audience, relates to the
    benefits and is compatible with the product?

5.  Write an attention-getting concept.

6.  Write the "memorable" line that evokes an emotional and
    buying response.

7.  Write a rhyming jingle that mentions the product. A rhym-
    ing dictionary is one of your tools.

8.  What artist(s) can best project the "mood" of the jingle?

Write this suggestion in a brief paragraph below the jingle. State why you think they are most suitable. Remember to say "a singer like" or "a group like." This proves you are budget conscious, flexible and objective.

9. Write a middle or closing *spoken* selling message. Not all jingles can stand alone.

# One Shining Hour (The technique ▪43▪ of writing the quiz and audience-participation shows)

The writer will probably find the least satisfaction in preparing the material that is presented on these shows. The shows are mostly spontaneous and nothing can be written except what is called the "routine sheet." The script will have a written opening and closing, introductions, and what are presumed to be ad-lib jokes but most of the time are not.

If the program is a quiz program, the questions and answers are written out in advance. In some instances, even the participants are given written material, which means that the show has been rehearsed and isn't what it seems at all. If you watch, you will see an acknowledgment of this at the end of the show before or after the credits are rolled.

The most important consideration is the personality of the host or master of ceremonies of the program. The writer must get to him or her and everything that is written is done in consultation with and with the consent of the central personality. This is no disparagement of game or quiz show MC's. They must be attractive, alert, communicative with all types of personalities and constantly aware of the floor manager and the producer. The MC is a very special kind of entertainer and this is why the successful writer of a quiz or audience-participation show should try to develop a close rapport with the central personality.

Quiz shows can be fun for the writer who likes to research historical facts, psychological opinions or trivia. It's an added asset if you are tuned in to the type of humor the central figure enjoys and write for and to that.

Don't be disillusioned if you discover that the contestants on an audience-participation show are prepicked.

It was once my job to walk down the line of the audience as they waited to get in and talk with the people. I had to look for the enthusiastic person who wouldn't fall apart in front of a camera or freeze up. I would then report back to the producer with my list of names or descriptions. Sometimes, I was instructed to tell people that they were to be chosen. On other shows, I merely reported back without saying anything and the look of surprise and pleasure of the chosen contestants was genuine.

Certain quiz shows screen contestants before they are selected. People write in and say they would like to appear; they are called and given careful scrutiny as to appearance, self-confidence, scope of general knowledge and emotional stability. Those who "pass" are invited to appear and scheduled far in advance.

The creators of game shows are a wonder to me, but unless the game show is one of questions and answers, the writer is not involved in much more than writing a routine sheet of what happens when. Frankly, I find this a colossal bore.

Watch a quiz show or question-and-answer game show. Take notes on the continuity, even the commercial breaks. Time the segments. Keep a count of the number of questions and answers. Write a routine sheet for a game show.

Write questions and answers for a quiz show and remember to include the opening and closing segments, the introductions and a joke or two that the MC will find compatible with his personality and can deliver with ease.

That may not be the end of it. If the unit is understaffed—and it often is if the show is locally produced on an independent station that has no network affiliation—the writer may find himself with the job of informing the contestants that the prizes they have won are taxable. In certain instances, the contestant discovers that he must pay for the delivery of the prize; the prize is no longer available and a lesser substitute is made or the contestant simply does not receive that which he "won" in that shining hour of triumph.

This is really no one's fault. Manufacturers and/or dealers furnish prizes for the publicity they receive for the mention of their product. Most are ethical, but if the writer, responsible for obtaining the prizes, then goes through the painful process of exchanging correspondence with an irate and disappointed contestant who does not receive the expected prizes, it can be most unpleasant. This can go on for months and is very time-consuming. Some arrangement is usually made with a persistent contestant, but it's an unpleasant experience for everyone. If the writer has to deal with the acquisition of prizes and the manufacturer fails to honor his commitment, report at once to the producer who will notify the legal department. You'll still have to deal with the problem, probably, unless it gets into litigation, but at least never approach a manufacturer or dealer who has welched on his agreement, and give him a chance to do it again. I once spent eighteen months in correspondence with a woman who had "won" a new wardrobe and received nothing. Writing is sometimes not just program material. Try not to be the person who has to acquire the "prizes" for the program, but if it's your assignment, you're stuck with it. See the merchandise and try to get it delivered to the studio before the program is aired. Don't accept a telephoned promise. Make an appointment and go to see the "prize." Get the donor to sign a form that may say:

> Sturdy, Inc. agrees to donate one Stiraround Washing Machine to station WXYZ to a winning contestant on the Home Folks Show.
>
> *Signature*
> Title

There is very little difference in a quiz show and game show routine sheet. I am not asking you to do anything I haven't done, so I am giving you the routine sheets of a quiz show and a game show that I viewed recently. Oddly enough, even the game shows seem to be part quiz, but let's look at the routine sheet for a quiz show where they don't roll dice, shoot darts or race around with a peanut on their noses.

This familiar and very popular quiz show has a host, a panel of nine celebrities and two guest participants. Points are awarded for correct answers. First, the routine sheet and then typical questions.

| SEGMENT | TIME |
| --- | --- |
| INTRO PANELISTS AND GUESTS | 0:45 |
| COMMERCIAL #1 | 0:05 |
| COMMERCIAL #2 | 0:30 |
| COMMERCIAL #3 | 0:15 |
| COMMERCIAL #4 | 0:10 |
| QUESTIONS | 4:00 |
| COMMERCIAL #5 | 0:30 |
| COMMERCIAL #6 | 0:30 |
| ANNC PRIZES | 1:30 |
| COMMERCIAL #7 | 0:30 |
| COMMERCIAL #8 | 0:30 |
| QUESTIONS | 4:00 |
| ANNC PRIZES | 1:00 |

| | |
|---|---|
| QUESTIONS | 3:00 |
| COMMERCIAL #9 | 0:30 |
| COMMERCIAL #10 | 0:30 |
| COMMERCIAL #11 | 0:30 |
| NEWS PROMO | 0:45 |
| QUESTIONS | 3:00 |
| GRAND PRIZE AWARD | 1:00 |
| PROMO PANEL ACTIVITIES | 1:00 |
| GENERAL PRIZE AWARD | 0:30 |
| WRAP-UP | 0:20 |
| CREDITS | 0:30 |
| PROGRAM TITLE AND LOGO | 0:25 |

## TYPICAL QUESTIONS ON A QUIZ SHOW

1.   One of television's superstars wrote an autobiography titled —*Always on Sunday* . . . Who was it?

2.   What do you first put on a fruit stain on clothing?

3.   A popular singer had two big hits that outsold all others— the songs were "Too Much Too Late" and "It's Not For Me To Say." Who is the singer?

4.   Elizabeth Taylor had it, gave it up and wants it back. What is it?

5.   Does pain hurt more in the dark?

6.   Who was the youngest man to be president of the United States?

You must always have more questions than there will be time for in case the host, the panelists or the audience gives away the answer or one of the contestants is given credit for a correct answer that is challenged or proved wrong. You'll find the material for these questions in many places. If you're a trivia nut, you'll have a wonderful time.

The only way you can learn about routine sheets and the kinds of questions to be written is to sit down and watch a quiz show and carefully time the program segments, commercials and other insertions.

If time is running out, a panelist goes on an ego trip or a contestant is slow, you may see some "up-cutting" (the abrupt cutoff of a program to start a commercial or the abrupt cutoff of one commercial to start another commercial). Learn the term *up-cutting*. There's a lot of it. As a writer, you have nothing to do with that. It's all happening in the control room. But as a writer, if you have

written a timeless last line on a commercial and it's "cut off" by
the start of another commercial, don't say anything to your creative director or the account executive who handles that product
in your agency. The account executive has already had twenty
threatening phone calls from the advertiser and the station or
network has had twenty calls from the account executive asking for
a "make good" (the rescheduling of a commercial in a time slot for
TOTAL replay but without additional payment of money). Watch
the quiz shows; count the number of commercials and time them
as well as those few moments actually given to the questions.

A routine sheet for a game show is not much different. Notice
that the MC must be a real time-watcher. Those commercials have
to be in there at a scheduled time. Most game show MC's are so
smooth, they never have to muzzle a contestant, but it does happen. Watch here for "up-cutting" in case some contestant has a lot
of relatives in the audience and wants to name all of them.

A game show can be anything from guessing prices of merchandise, word association, dice rolling, pulling levers on a table to
make balls fall into certain holes that are symbols of certain prizes
or a myriad of other stunts designed for audience participation.

Here is a typical game show routine sheet.

| SEGMENT | TIME |
|---|---|
| INTRO PLAYERS/GAME EXPLANATION | 0:15 |
| MULTIPLE CHOICE QUESTION AND ANSWERS | 3:00 |
| CHAT AND GAME | 2:00 |
| COMMERCIAL #1 | 0:30 |
| COMMERCIAL #2 | 0:30 |
| GAME | 3:00 |
| PRIZE DISPLAY | 1:00 |
| GAME | 3:00 |
| COMMERCIAL #3 | 0:30 |
| COMMERCIAL #4 | 0:30 |
| COMMERCIAL #5 | 0:30 |
| COMMERCIAL #6 | 0:30 |
| GAME | 3:00 |
| PRIZES | 0:15 |
| GAME | 1:40 |
| PRIZES | 0:30 |
| GAME | 0:45 |
| COMMERCIAL #7 | 0:30 |
| COMMERCIAL #8 | 0:30 |
| COMMERCIAL #9 | 0:30 |

| COMMERCIAL #10 | 0:30 |
| GAME | 2:30 |
| COMMERCIAL #11 | 0:30 |
| COMMERCIAL #12 | 0:20 |

All of this was followed by a one-minute good-bye and a fast roll of credits and program logo of slightly under a minute. In this instance, I could only conclude that the MC did not really have the show under control. I watched it for several days and the program segments varied in length of time, partly because of the nature of the game, the lack of control of the contestants and the obvious zeal on the part of the producer that all twelve commercials were going to get on and be rolled from start to finish.

If all of these commercial breaks turn you off now that you've seen the number on paper, sit in front of your television set and time the show yourself. Most game shows are played in the morning before the soaps start in the afternoon.

Do not be disillusioned, friend. Television is a profit-making business. If you think anything else, you're going to get hurt.

# ▪44▪   The Writer's Future

There was a time when the beginning writer aspired to work on what is called educational television or public television. The idealistic communications students of the late sixties and early seventies felt that their creativity could best be expressed in the quality programming of those stations. While this was and is a commendable aspiration, writers must realize that the "network" of educational or public television stations is constantly holding telethons for funds. If a position on such a station becomes an actual experience, the writer and everyone else will find himself very underpaid.

A greater frustration comes with the discovery that much of the programming is imported. The performing unions in the United States have strongly opposed the importation of such programs as *Upstairs, Downstairs* not for lack of excellence but because they are produced abroad with foreign actors who are paid much less than the American performer. Certain corporations fund concerts, live ballet performances and other cultural events, but these programs offer little if any opportunity to the writer.

Most recently, writers talk of the wonderful opportunities that cable, pay television, satellites and disc television and even a fourth network will give to the writer. Cable television offers some limited activity for the writer; pay television is usually a sporting event or special movie and satellites merely make possible farther distance transmission of programs from a sister station from another city that is owned by the same shareholders. Disc television, which is just now beginning to reach the market, is largely old movies, new movies or stockpiled programs that people cherish and like to see over and over again. This will grow.

According to the experts who are concerned with these technological developments, it will be another five years before these plans are a reality for most families. While the writer must watch for opportunities in these areas, the immediate opportunities lie in the local stations, the networks and the production companies.

As for the much-yearned-for fourth network, this requires two C's, capital and courage. Somehow the stranglehold that the networks have on the stations must be broken. Stations must have fluidity of choice. As it is, few acquisitions are made. Stations merely change affiliation and try to go with the current leader in the ratings or the network with the fattest wallet. Few cities have seven channels. Some have only two, each of which is a primary affiliate of one network with an option to carry programs from another. The pressure of the network holding the primary affiliation to carry their programs hardly makes it comfortable for the station manager even if he feels his community would respond better to a program transmitted by another network. Syndication is cutting into network dominance.

The fourth network is not yet in sight, so the writer should put away his dreams of that opportunity.

There is some light on the path. The Federal Communications Commission is considering limiting clear channel radio stations, whose signal reaches for many miles. According to the proposal, clear channels must give up some of their power and more channels would be allocated for FM stations. If this proposal, which is being fought bitterly by the clear channel stations, becomes a reality, there may be more opportunities for writers on these FM stations of limited reach. How they will be programmed is unpredictable, but there's a chance, especially if the writer has more than one area of expertise such as engineering or salesmanship.

The writer should never spurn the UHF (ultrahigh frequency) station that operates on channels 14 to 83. The usual channels 2 to 13 are called VHF, or very high frequency stations. The VHF has more power and more coverage and therefore reaches more people than a UHF. A VHF will extend its physical power in a radius of seventy-five to eighty miles, while a UHF usually extends in a radius of forty-five to sixty-five miles. For a long time, television sets did not have UHF channels, but set manufacturers are now required to build sets that provide for the reception of UHF stations. The only problem with that is, some people buy sets that provide UHF channels but do not have adaptors that make it possible for them to receive UHF programs.

At last, the UHF station is coming into its own, and while many of them have network affiliation, some of them don't. There are even some all UHF markets in the country but they are few. National sales representatives are no longer even asked if a station is VHF or UHF. If a buyer in an ad agency wants his client's product in a certain market, he will buy time in that market whether the station is VHF or UHF. It used to be virtually impossible to sell UHF to anyone, but that time has passed.

Even if the market has a strong VHF with a network affiliation, the UHF station can be an important competitor with good management and a fine inventory. That inventory is programming. Some of it is purchased from syndicators, some comes from the network if the UHF station has a network affiliation and some of it is produced locally.

Don't refuse a job on a UHF station. Try to be a local salesperson as well as a writer. Charlie, the local car salesman, may not be the greatest television personality, but if you can sell him time and write a commercial that sounds like Charlie, you have a job. Check first with the station manager, because you must first convince him that you can sell and then let him find out that you are a writer. You are looking for experience and if you can establish a good record at a UHF station, you can move on to other areas in television.

You'll just have to wait for those promised technological developments that seemingly hold so much hope for the creative person.

# ▪ 45 ▪     How to Get a Job

If you have followed all of the assignments in this book, you now have a job-hunting portfolio. It belongs to you.

If you plan to work in an agency, shoot for the top. Know the names of the big agencies, those with branches all over the country, and begin there. Telephone for the name of the creative director(s). Lie. Tell the operator that you are Clancy or Clara Hooper of the Telecom Agency in Someother City, State, and you would like to put the creative director(s)' name on your mailing list of outstanding writers in the country. Don't make the call from a phone booth where you will be interrupted with "Please deposit five cents," and don't make it from your home unless you plan to startle the dry cleaner by answering the phone "Telecom." Rent a hotel room for two or three days, because after all, you're in town for only a few days, remember? You can try telephoning from home and asking for the name of the creative director(s) and the operator may give it to you, but most of the time she will not, since all creative directors have wall-to-wall portfolios.

The first thing for you to realize is that not all jungles are in Africa. You are entering a highly competitive field.

Once you have the name of the creative director, write or preferably call for an appointment. Tell the truth about why you want the appointment. Some creative directors will see you, others won't. Many will tell you to drop your book off and they'll take a look at it. This is why it is important to have duplicate books. You have to have something to carry around with you while you leave one, and be prepared to wait a very long time for the creative director to look at your book and either call you to come in or write you a polite letter and tell you to pick it up. A month is long enough to wait.

If you find that you cannot get an appointment with the creative director, call every day about 12:30 or 1:00 when he's out to lunch. Don't leave a message. Just tell the operator to tell him you called. Do this daily for three weeks, then call him about 9:30 A.M. By this time, he is familiar with your name and will talk with you. If he tells you there are no openings, ask him if you can come in with your book and get his advice and opinion. Stated that way, you usually get in to see the great one. Many large agencies have training programs for secretaries and clerical workers who want to become writers. Even if you're already a writer, take the clerical job, get into the group, show the book you've done at the appropriate moment, but listen carefully to every word that is being taught you. They are teaching you their way of doing things. If you don't make it into the junior copywriter category, keep your eye peeled for another job. Be prepared to accept a small salary and if you can live at home and chip in for rent and groceries, it's a lot better than sharing a shabby apartment (if you can find one) with three or four other people. A writer needs time alone as well as security of sorts until he is established. There's nothing wrong with living at home with your parents, but don't forget to pay something.

Watch the newspapers carefully. You will not see many jobs for television writers listed in the classified section. For this reason, you must use the same technique that you would use for the agency, for the local station or the flagship station of a network. Find out the name of the station manager and make an appointment. Start at the top. You will be referred down the line to the program director or to the director of news. Listen a lot and say little. If you have to explain your portfolio, you haven't done a good job.

Unfortunately, there are some agencies who will look at any book offered to them. They are not looking for an employee. They are looking for ideas. Yours. There is really no way to protect yourself from these few unscrupulous agencies, but a second or a third book is of some help if you see your idea on the screen or recognize a provable adaptation. You cannot copyright an idea.

Contacts is the name of the game and keep all of them superficial and affable. Never feud with anyone and keep all contacts active during your entire career. Always remember to drop a note of thanks to a creative director, station manager, program director or to anyone who gives you his time for a personal interview.

If you have a relative in the business and are offered a job, take it. You'll have to live with the resentment of your co-workers, but that won't matter if you are doing what you like to do.

Sometimes, the fastest way into the business is to go to bed with someone who can hire you. It's also the fastest way out. Sex is here to stay, I think, and women are not the only ones who are importuned for favors. Agencies and networks are full of never-married or divorced women executives who began as lovers of executives who have given them a title in return for past favors, but abandoned them as they climbed the executive ladder. These women often spot a young unmarried or married executive and invent a piece of business that *must* be discussed over a drink at the end of the day. You're on your own.

If she tires of you or you of her, she could do you a lot of harm and retard or seriously damage your career. If you want to avoid this, always have to catch a train; have an engagement; but keep it platonic with an occasional lunch. Tread carefully. There was once a very competent writer who never received a promotion and her explanation was that she had never slept with the right people despite her rather thorough search.

The business is full of politics, ranging from petty speculative or true gossip about co-workers to planned hatchet jobs. Never disclose any details of your personal life; never choose up sides in a power struggle; say, "Hmm," a lot; never repeat anything you've been told; never complain about a co-worker or superior and be a bore by constantly talking business during business hours. Never have more than two drinks with a co-worker or superior and develop a hobby that fills in the gaps in conversation. If you are criticized or "chewed out," listen; keep a smile on your face; agree that you've erred if you have; don't defend yourself if you haven't; be polite; answer softly with "I understand" and thank the person for calling it to your attention. Then go home and kick a pillow around the room.

If you are fired, ask for a reference. You may get one that reads, "Paul Smith was employed by us as a writer from February 1 to October 1."

Once you have some experience, list it on your résumé and never claim credit for something you didn't do. Above all, never take a reel or copy of someone else's work on interviews. They'll spot you as a fraud.

The one thing you must have is the motivation to pursue.

Avoid personnel departments. They are looking for clerical workers.

Face-to-face appointments with persons who can hire are always the best. It's too easy to write a letter and get back a no-no. There is seldom anything personal in a rejection, but if you are not psychologically fit to live in a world of rejection, insecurity and politics, television is not for you.

These are the facts as I know them. So take that portfolio, make those appointments; tell the truth during the interview; take that first job; keep on learning and climbing and one day you'll see your name on the credit crawl and maybe the rest of us will see you holding an Emmy for best writer of something or other. It has happened to people who don't write as well as you will once you've finished the assignments in this book.

It has been said there are no happy lives, only happy moments. The moments you spend in your job in television may be hectic and often unjust, but they will be tinged with happiness at worst, ecstasy at best, and your love for television will become an incurable disease a lot of people want to get.

Persistence is the password. Keep your portfolio and reel up to date. All writers should take a shopping bag with them on the day they report to work. Keep it in your desk. You'll need it for your personal things if a shuffle comes. Keep in touch with writers in other agencies, stations and networks and may your shopping bag rot in your desk or wear out as you move on and up.

# Index

147